SCOTT®

1991
FEDERAL AND STATE

DUCK STAMP

CATALOGUE

PRESIDENT — Wayne Lawrence
VICE PRESIDENT/PUBLISHER — Stuart J. Morrissey
EDITORIAL DIRECTOR — Richard L. Sine
EDITOR — William W. Cummings
ASSISTANT EDITOR — William H. Hatton
VALUING EDITOR — Martin J. Frankevicz
COMPUTER CONTROL COORDINATOR — Denise Oder
NEW ISSUE EDITOR — David C. Akin
VALUING ANALYST — Roger L. Listwan
EDITORIAL ASSISTANT — Beth Brown
ART/PRODUCTION DIRECTOR — Edward Heys
PRODUCTION COORDINATOR — Janine Skinn Apple
DIRECTOR OF MARKETING & SALES — Jeff Lawrence
SALES MANAGER — Mike Porter
ADVERTISING MANAGER — David Lodge

Copyright® 1990 by

Scott Publishing Co.

911 Vandemark Road, Sidney, Ohio 45365

A division of AMOS PRESS INC., publishers of
Linn's Stamp News, Coin World, Cars & Parts magazine and *The Sidney Daily News.*

MIGRATORY BIRD
HANDPAINTED
FIRST DAY COVERS

STATE ★ FEDERAL ★ FOREIGN

**FRED COLLINS
MILFORD CACHETS**
P.O. Box 5000, Hewitt, NJ 07421
Phone 201-853-7107

**MILFORD IS THE <u>ONLY</u> CACHETMAKER
DOING ALL STATE DUCKS FDCs.**

CONTENTS

1990 Colorado Companion Print

FREE

Receive one free companion print with every 1990 Colorado Duck Stamp Print ordered

Companion Print Specifications:
Edition Size
Signed and numbered
    companion print   950
Artist Proof Companion Print   95
Free Companion Print   Extent of
                   Colorado Sales

Image Size: 13"x18"
Retail Price:
Signed & Numbered Companion Print
                       $100.00
Artist Proof Companion Print $225.00
Colorado Companion Print FREE with purchase of 1990 Colorado Duck Stamp Print

Colorado Canada   Companion Print   Tom Hirata

The 1990 COMPANION PRINT IS BEING OFFERED EXCLUSIVELY THROUGH SPORT'EN ART DEALERS

Sport'en Art dealers have available full-size Colorado companion print to accompany the 1990 "First of State" Colorado Duck Stamp Print by Robert Steiner. The companion print entitled "Colorado Canadas" by Tom Hirata, is being offered exclusively through Sport'en Art dealers at no extra charge.

With the purchase of a Colorado Duck Stamp Print by Robert Steiner, you will receive, absolutely free, a companion print by Tom Hirata, entitled "Colorado Canadas". This free print is a special signed and

numbered Colorado companion edition which represents a $100.00 value.

"Colorado Canadas" will be issued as a companion print with matching numbers to the "First of State" Colorado prints. For instance, if you have print number 2000/14,500 the companion print will be numbered CC2000. The companion print is also available as a limited edition print with the edition size of 950. An Artist Proof edition is also available with a color remarque in an edition of 95.

1990 "First of State" Colorado Duck Stamp Print

High Plains Honkers   Robert Steiner

Robert Steiner's beautiful painting "High Plains Honkers" has been chosen by the Colorado Division of Wildlife and Colorado Ducks Unlimited as a winning design for the 1990 Colorado "First of State" Duck Stamp and print. Revenues derived from the sale of these prints and stamps will be used to acquire and enhance wetlands for waterfowl habitat.

	1990 First of State
Colorado DSP Specifications:	
Edition Size:	
Regular Edition	14,500
Medallion Edition	2,000
Executive Edition	450
Governor's Edition	700
Image Size	6"x9
Retail Price:	
Regular Edition	$169.00
Medallion Edition	$319.00
Executive Edition	$519.00
Governor's Edition	$619.00

All print prices listed above include a mint and an artist's signed regular stamp.

FOR MORE INFORMATION
PLEASE CONTACT:

THE DEPOT LTD.
R.R. 3
SULLIVAN, IL 61951
1-800-223-3768

Dealer inquires welcome contact:
Sport'en Art/1-800-382-5723

FEDERAL AND STATE DUCK STAMPS

"License" is a more accurate term to use when defining these items than is the word "stamps." Like the postage stamp, Federal and State Duck stamps allow the purchaser to pre-pay for the right to a service. In the case of the postage stamp, that service is the transport of an envelope or parcel to its destination. Duck stamps show the user as a licensed hunter.

Items shown in this book are required for the hunting of waterfowl, but it not necessarily limited to that role. There are items listed herein, issued by some states, which permit the user to hunt a variety of game.

This catalogue is broken into three principal types of listings: items issued by the U.S. federal government, items issued by individual states, and items issued by other governmental agencies not considered federal or statewide. Included in the listings are every verifiable item we learned of from our array of experts.

The collecting of State and Federal Duck Stamps is a greatly developing hobby. The body of knowledge continues to grow, and it is a safe assumption that the release of this first-ever catalogue will spark additional research — which, in turn, will lead to future additions and modifications to the listings.

For the most part, the items shown in this catalogue are collected in an unused form, except where that is an impossibility or when the cost differential between a used and unused item is too great for an individual collector to justify. There is no "right" or "wrong" way to collect duck stamps. The later state duck stamps are quite attractive miniature pieces of art. Earlier stamps were more functional than beautiful. They did, however, do the same job.

ACKNOWLEDGEMENTS

Appreciation and gratitude go to the following individuals who have assisted us in preparing information included in this catalogue. These individuals have generously shared their knowledge with others through the medium of this work. Those whose names follow have provided information that is in addition to the many dealer price lists and advertisements and other information which was used in producing the *Scott 1991 Federal and State Duck Stamp Catalogue*. Support from these people goes beyond data leading to catalogue values, for they also are key to the depth of the listings.

David H. Curtis	Thomas DeLuca	Reuben Klein	E.L. Vanderford
Charles Deaton	Bob Dumaine	David R. Torre	Carlo Vechiarelli

Special thanks are extended to Jim Drake of Sidney, Ohio, who permitted us to photograph his hand-carved and painted Canvasback decoy replica for the front cover. Drake has been carving ducks for 12 years.

HOW TO USE THIS BOOK

CATALOGUE VALUE

The Scott Catalogue value is a retail price, what you could expect to pay for the stamp in a grade of Fine-Very Fine. The value listed is a reference which reflects recent actual dealer selling prices. Dealer retail price lists, public auction results, published prices in advertising, and individual solicitation of retail prices from dealers have been used in establishing the values found in this catalogue.

Use this catalogue as a guide in your own buying and selling. The actual price you pay for a stamp may be higher or lower than the catalogue value because of one or more of the following: the amount of personal service a dealer offers, increased interest in the state or artist represented by the stamp, whether an item is a "loss leader," part of a special sale, or otherwise is being sold for a short period of time at a lower price, or if at a public auction you are able to obtain an item inexpensively because of little interest in the item at that time.

Fine ⟶

SCOTT
CATALOGUES
VALUE STAMPS
IN THIS GRADE

Fine-Very Fine ⟶

Very Fine ⟶

GRADE

A stamp's grade and condition are crucial to its value. Values quoted in this catalogue are for stamps graded at Fine-Very Fine and with no faults. Exceptions are noted in the text. The accompanying illustrations show an example of a Fine-Very Fine grade between the grades immediately below and above it: Fine and Very Fine.

FINE stamps have the design noticeably off-center on two sides. Imperforate stamps may have small margins. Used stamps may have heavier than usual cancellations.

FINE-VERY FINE stamps may be somewhat off-center on one side, or only slightly off-center on two sides. Signatures on used stamps will not detract from the design. This is the grade used to establish Scott Catalogue values.

VERY FINE stamps may be slightly off-center on one side, with the design well clear of the edge. Imperforate stamps will have three margins at least normal size. Used stamps will have light or otherwise neat cancellations.

CONDITION

The above definitions describe *grade*, which is centering and (for used stamps) effect of marking/signature. *Condition* refers to the soundness of the stamp, i.e., faults, repairs, and other factors influencing price.

Copies of a stamp which are of a lesser grade and/or condition trade at lower prices. Those of exceptional quality often command higher prices.

Factors that can increase the value of a stamp include exceptionally wide margins, particularly fresh color, and the presence of selvage.

Factors other than faults that decrease the value of a stamp include no gum on stamps issued with gum, regumming, hinge remnant, foreign object adhering to gum, straight edge on stamps originally perforated on four sides, or natural inclusion.

Faults include a missing piece, tear, clipped perforation, pin or other hole, surface scuff, thin spot, crease, toning, oxidation or other form of color changeling, short of pulled perforation, stains or such man-made changes as reperforation or the chemical removal or lightening of a cancellation.

Scott Publishing Co. recognizes that there is no formal, enforced grading scheme for postage stamps, and that the final price you pay for a stamp or obtain for a stamp you are selling will be determined by individual agreement at the time of the transaction.

UNDERSTANDING THE LISTINGS

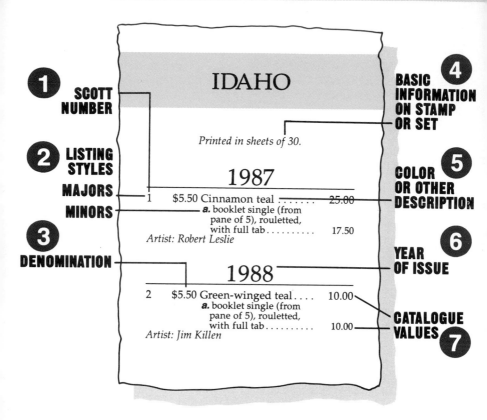

Above is a "typical" listing from this catalogue. Following are detailed explanations of each of the highlighted parts of the listing.

1 **Scott number** — Stamp collectors use Scott numbers to identify specific stamps when buying, selling, or trading stamps, and for ease in organizing their collections. Each State and Federal Duck Stamp issued has a unique number within its category. Therefore, Idaho Scott 2 can only refer to a single stamp. Although the Scott Catalogue usually lists stamps in chronological order by date of issue, when a set of stamps is issued over a period of time, the stamps within that set are kept together without regard of date of issue. This follows the normal collecting approach of keeping stamps in their natural sets.

The "RW" prefix for the Federal Duck Stamps is drawn from the larger Scott cataloguing system. The State Duck Stamps do not have a prefix.

2 **Listing styles** — there are two principal types of catalogue listings: major and minor.

Majors normally are in a larger type style than minor listings. They also may be distinguished by having as their catalogue number a numeral with or without a capital-letter suffix and with or without a prefix.

Minors are in a smaller type style and have a small-letter suffix (or, only have the small letter itself shown if the listing is immediately beneath its major listing). These listings show a variety of the "normal," or major item. Examples include the booklet version of a stamp when the major variety is ˙issued in sheets, or a change in the type of serial number.

3 **Denomination** — normally the face value of the stamp, i.e., the cost of the stamp from the issuing agency at the time of issue. When the denomination is shown in parentheses, it does not appear on the stamp.

4 **Basic information on stamp or set** — introducing each stamp issue, this section normally includes the method of presentation, q.v., sheets of 30, and sometimes additional information. Dates of issue are as precise as Scott is able to confirm.

5 **Color or other description** — this line provides information to solidify identification of the stamp. Historically, in stamp catalogues, when stamps normally were printed in a single color, only the color appeared here. With modern printing techniques, which include multicolor presses which mix inks on the paper, earlier methods of color identification are no longer applicable. In this book, the identity of the subject of a pictorial stamp is noted.

6 **Year of issue** — in stamp sets issued over more than one year, the number in parentheses signifies the year the single stamp appeared. Stamps without a date appeared during the first year of the span. Dates are not always given for minor varieties.

7 **Value unused** and **Value used** — the catalogue values are based on stamps which are in a grade of Fine-Very Fine. Unused values refer to items which have not seen the duty for which they were intended. For gummed stamps, complete gum is expected. Stamps issued without gum are noted. Unused values are for never-hinged stamps. Information about catalogue values shown in italics may be found in the following section, "Understanding Valuing Notations."

Federal Hunting Permit stamps are valued as unused (value to the left) and used (value to the right), while all values for state and other governmental issues are for unused stamps only.

UNDERSTANDING
VALUING NOTATIONS

A dash in the value column means that the stamp is known in a stated form or variety, but information is lacking or insufficient for purposes of establishing a catalogue value.

Stamp values in *italics* generally refer to items which are difficult to value accurately. For expensive items, i.e., value at $1,000 or more, a value in italics represent an item which trades very seldom, such as a unique item. For inexpensive items, a value in italics represents a warning. An example is a single item with a very low face value which sells in the marketplace, at the time of issue, at an extreme multiple of face value.

EXAMINATION

Scott Publishing Co. will not pass upon the genuineness, grade or condition of stamps, because of the time and responsibility involved. Neither can Scott Publishing Co. appraise or identify philatelic material. The Company cannot take responsibility for unsolicited stamps.

ILLUSTRATIONS

All items in this catalogue are depicted actual size unless otherwise indicated.

Issued in panes of 28 subjects
Engraved: Flat Plate Printing

1934

Inscribed "Void after June 30, 1935"
Unwmk. *Perf. 11*
RW1 $1 blue (Mallards
   alighting) 400.00 85.00
   P# block of 6 .... 6,000.
   a. Imperf. pair .... 4,000.
   b. Vertical pair, imperf.
   horizontally .... —
Artist: J.N. "Ding" Darling
Quantity issued: 635,001

1935

Inscribed "Void after June 30, 1936"
RW2 $1 rose lake
   (Canvasbacks) 400.00 100.00
   P# block of 6 .... 7,000.
Artist: F.W. Benson
Quantity issued: 448,204

1936

Inscribed "Void after June 30, 1937"
RW3 $1 brown black
   (Canada geese) 200.00 50.00
   P# block of 6 .... 2,500.
Artist: R.E. Bishop
Quantity issued: 603,623

1937

Inscribed "Void after June 30, 1938"
RW4 $1 light green
(Greater scaup) 160.00 27.50
P# block of 6 .... 1,750.
Artist: J.D. Knap
Quantity issued: 783,039

1938

Inscribed "Void after June 30, 1939"
RW5 $1 light violet
(Pintails alighting) . 160.00 35.00
P# block of 6 .... 1,800.
Artist: Roland Clark
Quantity issued: 1,002,715

1939

Inscribed "Void after June 30, 1940"
RW6 $1 chocolate (Green-
winged teal) 115.00 15.00
P# block of 6 .... 1,200.
Artist: Lynn B. Hunt
Quantity issued: 1,111,561

1940

Inscribed "Void after June 30, 1941"
RW7 $1 sepia (Black
duck) 110.00 15.00
P# block of 6 .... 1,100.
Artist: F.L. Jaques
Quantity issued: 1,260,810

1941

Inscribed "Void after June 30, 1942"
RW8 $1 brown carmine
(Ruddy ducks) 110.00   15.00
P# block of 6 .... 1,000.
Artist: E.R. Kalmback
Quantity issued: 1,439,967

1942

Inscribed "Void after June 30, 1943"
RW9 $1 violet brown
(Widgeon) 110.00   14.00
P# block of 6 .... 1,000.
Artist: A.L. Ripley
Quantity issued: 1,383,629

1943

Inscribed "Void after June 30, 1944"
RW10 $1 deep rose
(Wood ducks) 47.50   15.00
P# block of 6 .... 425.00
Artist: Walter E. Bohl
Quantity issued: 1,169,352

1944

Inscribed "Void after June 30, 1945"
RW11 $1 red orange (White-
fronted geese) 40.00   14.00
P# block of 6 .... 400.00
Artist: Walter A. Weber
Quantity issued: 1,487,029

1945

Inscribed "Void after June 30, 1946"
RW12 $1 black
          (Shovelers) 35.00   10.00
     P# block of 6 .... 225.00
Artist: Owen Gromme
Quantity issued: 1,725,505

1946

Inscribed "Void after June 30, 1947"
RW13 $1 red brown
          (Redheads) 32.50   9.00
     P# block of 6 .... 225.00
Artist: Robert W. Hines
Quantity issued: 2,016,841

1947

Inscribed "Void after June 30, 1948"
RW14 $1 black (Snow
          geese) 35.00   9.00
     P# block of 6 .... 225.00
Artist: Jack Murray
Quantity issued: 1,722,677

1948

Inscribed "Void after June 30, 1949"
RW15 $1 bright blue
          (Buffleheads) 32.50   9.00
     P# block of 6 .... 225.00
Artist: Maynard Reece
Quantity issued: 2,127,603

1949

Inscribed "Void after June 30, 1950"
RW16 $2 bright green
      (Goldeneyes) 32.50   8.00
    P# block of 6 . . . . 225.00
Artist: Roge E. Preuss
Quantity issued: 1,954,734

1950

Inscribed "Void after June 30, 1951"
RW17 $2 violet (Trumpeter
      swans) 45.00   7.00
    P# block of 6 . . . . 325.00
Artist: Walter A. Weber
Quantity issued: 1,903,644

1951

Inscribed "Void after June 30, 1952"
RW18 $2 gray black
      (Gadwalls) 45.00   5.00
    P# block of 6 . . . . 325.00
Artist: Maynard Reece
Quantity issued: 2,167,767

1952

Inscribed "Void after June 30, 1953"
RW19 $2 deep ultramarine
      (Harlequins) 45.00   5.00
    P# block of 6 . . . . 325.00
Artist: John H. Dick
Quantity issued: 2,296,628

1953

Inscribed "Void after June 30, 1954"
RW20 $2 dark rose brown
        (Blue-winged teal)   45.00   5.00
        P# block of 6 .... 325.00
Artist: C.B. Seagers
Quantity issued: 2,268,446

1954

Inscribed "Void after June 30, 1955"
RW21 $2 black (Ring-
            necked ducks) 45.00   4.75
        P# block of 6 .... 325.00
Artist: H.D. Sandstrom
Quantity issued: 2,184,550

1955

Inscribed "Void after June 30, 1956"
RW22 $2 dark blue (Blue
            geese) 45.00   4.75
        P# block of 6 .... 325.00
Artist: Stanley Stearns
Quantity issued: 2,369,940

1956

Inscribed "Void after June 30, 1957"
RW23 $2 black
            (Mergansers) 45.00   4.75
        P# block of 6 .... 325.00
Artist: E.J. Bierly
Quantity issued: 2,332,014

1957

Inscribed "Void after June 30, 1958"
RW24　$2 emerald
　　　(American Eider)　.　45.00　　4.75
　　P# block of 6 . . . . 325.00
Artist: J.M. Abbott
Quantity issued: 2,355,353

1958

Inscribed "Void after June 30, 1959"
RW25　$2 black (Canada
　　　geese) . . . .　45.00　　4.75
　　P# block of 6 . . . . 325.00
Artist: Leslie C. Kouba
Quantity issued: 2,176,425

Giori Press Printing.
Issued in panes of 30 subjects.

1959

Inscribed "Void after June 30, 1960"
RW26　$3 Labrador retriever
　　　with mallard . . . . .　60.00　　4.75
　　P# block of 4 . . . . 285.00
Artist: Maynard Reece
Quantity issued: 1,628,365

1960

Inscribed "Void after June 30, 1961"
RW27　$3 Redheads . . . . . .　60.00　　4.00
　　P# block of 4 . . . . 285.00
Artist: John A. Ruthven
Quantity issued: 1,727,534

1961

Inscribed "Void after June 30, 1962"
RW28 $3 Mallards 60.00   4.00
   P# block of 4 . . . . 285.00
Artist: E.A. Morris
Quantity issued: 1,346,003

1962

Inscribed "Void after June 30, 1963"
RW29 $3 Pintails landing   70.00   5.50
   P# block of 4 . . . . 350.00
Artist: E.A. Morris
Quantity issued: 1,147,553

1963

Inscribed "Void after June 30, 1964"
RW30 $3 Pacific brant . . .   65.00   5.50
   P# block of 4 . . . . 350.00
Artist: E.J. Bierly
Quantity issued: 1,455,486

1964

Inscribed "Void after June 30, 1965"
RW31 $3 Hawaiian nene
   geese 65.00   5.50
   P# block of 4 . . . . 2,250.
Artist: Stanley Stearns
Quantity issued: 1,573,155

1965

Inscribed "Void after June 30, 1966"
RW32 $3 Canvasbacks ... 65.00   5.50
  P# block of 4 .... 325.00
Artist: Ron Jenkins
Quantity issued: 1,558,755

1966

Inscribed "Void after June 30, 1967"
RW33 $3 Whistling
         swans 65.00   5.00
  P# block of 4 .... 300.00
Artist: Stanley Stearns
Quantity issued: 1,805,341

1967

Inscribed "Void after June 30, 1968"
RW34 $3 Old squaw
         ducks 65.00   5.00
  P# block of 4 .... 300.00
Artist: Leslie C. Kouba
Quantity issued: 1,934,697

1968

Inscribed "Void after June 30, 1969"
RW35 $3 Hooded
         mergansers 40.00   5.50
  P# block of 4 .... 200.00
Artist: C.G. Pritchard
Quantity issued: 1,837,139

1969

Inscribed "Void after June 30, 1970"
RW36 $3 White-winged
    scoters 40.00 4.50
  P# block of 4 .... 200.00
Artist: Maynard Reece
Quantity issued: 2,087,115

1970

Inscribed "Void after June 30, 1971"
Engraved & Lithographed
RW37 $3 Ross's geese 40.00 4.00
  P# block of 4 .... 200.00
Artist: E.J. Bierly
Quantity issued: 2,420,244

1971

Inscribed "Void after June 30, 1972"
RW38 $3 Three cinnamon
    teal 27.50 3.75
  P# block of 4 .... 140.00
Artist: Maynard Reece
Quantity issued: 2,428,647

1972

Inscribed "Void after June 30, 1973"
RW39 $5 Empress geese .. 17.00 3.75
  P# block of 4 .... 75.00
Artist: Arthur M. Cook
Quantity issued: 2,183,981

1973

Inscribed "Void after June 30, 1974"
RW40 $5 Steller's eiders .   17.00   3.75
  P# block of 4 . . . . 80.00
Artist: Lee LeBlanc
Quantity issued: 2,113,594

1974

Inscribed "Void after June 30, 1975"
RW41 $5 Wood ducks . . .   14.00   3.75
  P# block of 4 . . . . 62.50
Artist: David A. Maass
Quantity issued: 2,190,268

1975

Inscribed "Void after June 30, 1976"
RW42 $5 Canvasback
        decoy 12.00   3.75
  P# block of 4 . . . . 52.50
Artist: James L. Fisher
Quantity issued: 2,218,589

1976

Inscribed "Void after June 30, 1977"
Engraved
RW43 $5 Canada geese . .   9.50   3.75
  P# block of 4 . . . . 50.00
Artist: Alderson Magee
Quantity issued: 2,248,394

1977

Inscribed "Void after June 30, 1978"
Lithographed & Engraved
RW44 $5 Ross's geese 9.50   3.75
    P# block of 4 ....   50.00
Artist: Martin R. Murk
Quantity issued: 2,180,625

1978

Inscribed "Void after June 30, 1979"
RW45 $5 Merganser 9.50   3.75
    P# block of 6 ....   50.00
Artist: Albert Gilbert
Quantity issued: 2,196,758

1979

Inscribed "Void after June 30, 1980"
RW46 $7.50 Green-
        winged teal 12.00   4.00
    P# block of 4 ....   75.00
Artist: Ken Michaelson
Quantity issued: 2,209,572

1980

Inscribed "Void after June 30, 1981"
RW47 $7.50 Mallards 12.00   4.00
    P# block of 4 ....   75.00
Artist: Richard Plasschaert
Quantity issued: 2,103,021

1981

Inscribed "Void after June 30, 1982"
RW48 $7.50 Ruddy ducks   12.00   4.00
   P# block of 4 . . . .   75.00
Artist: John S. Wilson
Quantity issued: 1,940,578

1982

Inscribed "Void after June 30, 1983"
RW49 $7.50 Canvasbacks .   12.00   4.00
   P# block of 4 . . . .   55.00
Artist: David A. Maass
Quantity issued: 1,926,253

1983

Inscribed "Void after June 30, 1984"
RW50 $7.50 Pintails 12.00   4.00
   P# block of 4 . . . .   55.00
Artist: Phil Scholer
Quantity issued: 1,867,998

1984

Inscribed "Void after June 30, 1985"
RW51 $7.50 Widgeon 12.00   4.00
   P# block of 4 . . . .   55.00
Artist: W.C. Morris
Quantity issued: 1,913,509
After Scott RW51 became void, uncut sheets
of 120 (4 panes of 30 separated by gutters)
were overprinted in the margins and
auctioned. See Official Souvenir Items No. 7

1985

Inscribed "Void after June 30, 1986"
RW52 $7.50 Cinnamon
      teal 12.00   4.00
      P# block of 4 . . . . 55.00
Artist: Gerald Mobley

1986

Inscribed "Void after June 30, 1987"
RW53 $7.50 Fulvous
      duck 12.00   4.00
      P# block of 4 . . . . 55.00
      a. Black omitted . . . . —
Artist: Burton E. Moore, Jr.

1987

Inscribed "Void after June 30, 1988"
Perf. 11½ x 11
RW54 $10 Redheads 14.00   4.00
      P# block of 4 . . . . 65.00
Artist: Arthur G. Anderson

1988

Inscribed "Void after June 30, 1989"
RW55 $10 Snow goose . . . 14.00   4.00
      P# block of 4 . . . . 65.00
Artist: Daniel Smith

1989

Inscribed "Void after June 30, 1990"
RW56 $12.50 Lesser
       scaup 17.50   3.50
  P# block of 4 .... 125.00
Artist: Neal Anderson

1990

Inscribed "Void after June 30, 1991"
RW57 $12.50 Black-
       bellied whistling
       duck 25.00   3.50
  P# block of 4 .... 125.00
Artist: Jim Hautman

ALABAMA

Printed in sheets of 10.
Stamps are numbered serially.

1979

1 $5 Wood ducks (rouletted) . 9.00
Artist: Barbara Keel

1980

2 $5 Mallards 8.00
Artist: Wayne Spradley

1981

3 $5 Canada geese 8.00
Artist: Jack Deloney

1982

4 $5 Green-winged teal 8.00
Artist: Joe Michelet

1983

5     $5 Widgeon 15.00
Artist: John Lee

1984

6     $5 Buffleheads 15.00
Artist: William Morris

1985

7     $5 Wood ducks 15.00
Artist: Larry Martin

1986

8     $5 Canada geese 15.00
Artist: Danny W. Dorning

1987

9     $5 Pintails 18.00
Artist: Robert C. Knutson

1988

10     $5 Canvasbacks 11.00
Artist: John Warr

1989

11     $5 Hooded mergansers 8.00
Artist: Elaine Byrd

1985 Alaska Waterfowl Stamp

1986 Alaska Waterfowl Stamp

1987 Alaska Waterfowl Stamp

1988 Alaska Waterfowl Stamp

1985

1    $5 Emperor geese 14.50
Artist: Daniel Smith

1986

2    $5 Steller's eiders 11.00
Artist: James Meger

1987

3    $5 Spectacled eiders 9.00
    a. booklet single (from
    pane of 5), rouletted,
    with tab 20.00
Artist: Carl Branson

1988

4    $5 Trumpeter swan 8.00
    a. booklet single (from
    pane of 5), rouletted,
    with tab 10.00
Artist: Jim Beaudoin

$5

expires 1-31-90

1989 Alaska Waterfowl Stamp

Printed in sheets of 30.

1989

5	$5	Barrow's goldeneyes	8.00
	a.	booklet single (from pane of 5), rouletted, with tab	10.00

Artist: Richard Timm

Printed in sheets of 30.
Stamps are numbered serially.

1987

1	$5.50 Pintails	14.00
	a. booklet single (from pane of 5), with side tab and selvage	10.00

Artist: Daniel Smith

1988

2	$5.50 Green-winged teal . . .	8.00
	a. booklet single (from pane of 5), with side tab and selvage	9.00

Artist: Sherrie Russell

1989

3	$5.50 Cinnamon teal	8.00
	a. booklet single (from pane of 5), with side tab and selvage	9.00

Artist: Robert Steiner

ARKANSAS

Imperforate varieties
of these stamps are printer's proofs.

1981

1	$5.50 Mallards (from sheet of 30)	60.00
	a. booklet single (from pane of 30), serial numbers (110,001-200,000) on reverse ...	60.00
	b. booklet single, with top (3-part) tab	—

Artist: Lee LeBlanc

1982

2	$5.50 Wood ducks (from sheet of 10)	55.00
	a. booklet single (from pane of 10), serial numbers (110,001-200,000) on reverse ...	55.00

Artist: Maynard Reece

1983

3	$5.50 Green-winged teal (from sheet of 10)	55.00
	a. booklet single (from pane of 10) serial numbers (70,001-160,000) on reverse	*1750.*

Artist: David Maass

1984

4	$5.50 Pintails (from sheet of 10)	20.00
	a. booklet single (from pane of 10), serial numbers (25,001-100,000) on reverse ...	25.00

Artist: Larry Hayden

25

1985

5    $5.50 Mallards (from sheet
             of 10) 12.00
        a. booklet single (from
             pane of 10), serial
             numbers (25,001-
             100,000) on reverse ... 17.50
Artist: Ken Carlson

1986

6    $5.50 Mallards (from sheet
             of 10) 10.00
        a. booklet single (from
             pane of 10), serial
             numbers (25,001-
             100,000) on reverse ... 14.00
Artist: John P. Cowan

1987

7    $5.50 Wood ducks (from
             sheet of 10) 10.00
*This stamp was issued following an order of
the state Supreme Court restoring the fee level
of the preceding year. The resulting stamp was
released long after the 1987 season had ended.*

8    $7 Wood ducks (from sheet
          of 10) 10.00
        a. booklet single (from
             pane of 10), serial
             numbers (25,001-
             100,000) on reverse ... 12.00
Artist: Robert Bateman

1988

9    $5.50 Pintails (from sheet
             of 10) 9.50
See note following Scott 7.

10   $7 Pintails (from sheet
          of 10) 9.00
        a. booklet single (from-
             pane of 10), serial
             numbers (25,001-
             100,000) on reverse ... 10.00
Artist: Maynard Reece

1989

11    $7   Mallards (from sheet
of 10) 9.00
      a. booklet single (from
pane of 10), serial
numbers (25,001-
100,000) on reverse ...   10.00
Artist: Philip Crowe

*Printed in booklet panes of 5 stamps.
Issues through 1978 are self-adhesive.
Stamps are serially numbered.*

1971

1	$1 Pintails	800.00

Artist: Paul Johnson
Shown at 85% of original size

1972

2	$1 Canvasbacks	3000.

Artist: Paul Johnson
Shown at 85% of original size

1973

3	$1 Mallards	14.00

Artist: Paul Johnson
Shown at 85% of original size

1974

4	$1 White-fronted geese	4.50

Artist: Paul Johnson
Shown at 85% of original size

1975

5    $1 Green-winged teal, on backing
paper with red wavy lines
(with gum "bleed" to front
of stamp, resulting in spotted or blotchy effect) 35.00
    a. waxy backing paper
      without red wavy lines
      (no gum "bleed") 100.00

Artist: Paul Johnson
Shown at 85% of original size

1976

6    $1 Widgeon, on backing paper
with red wavy lines (with
gum "bleed" to front of
stamp, resulting in spotted
or blotchy effect) 15.00
    a. waxy backing paper
      without red wavy lines
      (no gum "bleed") .....   —

Artist: Paul Johnson
Shown at 85% of original size

1977-78

7    $1 Cinnamon teal 55.00
8    $5 Cinnamon teal ('78) 8.50
Artist: Paul Johnson
Shown at 85% of original size

1978

9    $5 Hooded mergansers 145.00
Artist: Ken Michaelson
Shown at 85% of original size

CALIFORNIA

1979

10    $5 Wood ducks 7.50
Artist: Walter Wolfe

1980

11    $5 Pintails 7.00
Artist: Walter Wolfe

1981

12    $5 Canvasbacks 7.50
Artist: Robert Steinert

1982

13    $5 Widgeon 7.50
Artist: Robert Richert

1983

14 $5 Green-winged teal 7.50
Artist: Charles Allen

1984

15 $7.50 Mallard decoy 10.00
Artist: Robert Montanucci

1985

16 $7.50 Ring-necked duck 10.00
Artist: Richard Wilson

1986

17 $7.50 Canada goose 10.00
Artist: Sherrie Russell

1987

18    $7.50 Redheads 10.00
Artist: Robert Steiner

1988

19    $7.50 Mallards 10.00
Artist: Paul B. Johnson

1989

20    $7.50 Cinnamon teal 10.00
Artist: Robert Steiner

1990

1    $5 Widgeon 8.00
Artist: Robert Steiner

DELAWARE

Printed in sheets of 10 stamps.

1980

| 1 | $5 Black ducks . . . . | 95.00 |

Artist: Ned Mayne

1981

| 2 | $5 Snow geese . . . . | 85.00 |

Artist: Charles Rowe

1982

| 3 | $5 Canada geese . . . . | 90.00 |

Artist: Lois Butler

1983

| 4 | $5 Canvasbacks . . . . | 55.00 |

Artist: John Green

1984

5    $5 Mallards 22.50
Artist: Nolan Haan

1985

6    $5 Pintail 12.50
Artist: Don Breyfogle

1986

7    $5 Widgeon 10.00
Artist: Robert Leslie

1987

8    $5 Redheads 8.00
Artist: Bruce Langton

DELAWARE

1988

9    $5 Wood ducks 8.00
Artist: James Hautman

1989

10    $5 Buffleheads 7.50
Artist: Robert Leslie

1990

11    $5 Green-winged teal 7.50
Artist: Francis E. Sweet

36

1979

1    $3.25 Green-winged teal,
      booklet single (from
      pane of 5) 200.00
        a. with tab 220.00
Artist: Bob Binks
Shown at 70% of original size

1980

2    $3.25 Pintails, booklet
      single (from pane of 5) . .   30.00
        a. with tab 35.00
Artist: Ernest Simmons
Shown at 70% of original size

1981

3    $3.25 Widgeon, booklet
      single (from pane of 5) . .   30.00
        a. with tab 35.00
Artist: Clark Sullivan

1982

4    $3.25 Ring-necked duck,
      booklet single (from
      pane of 5) 45.00
        a. with tab 50.00
Artist: Lee Cable

1983

5    $3.25 Buffleheads, booklet
single (from pane of 5) .. 65.00
a. with tab 70.00

Artist: Heiner Hertling

1984

6    $3.25 Hooded merganser,
booklet single (from
pane of 5) 20.00
a. with tab 22.50

Artist: John Taylor

1985

7    $3.25 Wood duck, booklet
single (from pane of 5) .. 18.00
a. with tab 20.00

Artist: Bob Binks

1986

8    $3 Canvasbacks, single
(from sheet of 10) 10.00
        a. with tab 25.00

Artist: Robert Steiner

1987

9    $3.50 Mallards, single (from
sheet of 10) 7.00
        a. with tab 20.00

Artist: Ronald J. Louque

1988

10    $3.50 Redheads, single
(from sheet of 10) 6.00
        a. with tab 20.00

Artist: Ronald J. Louque

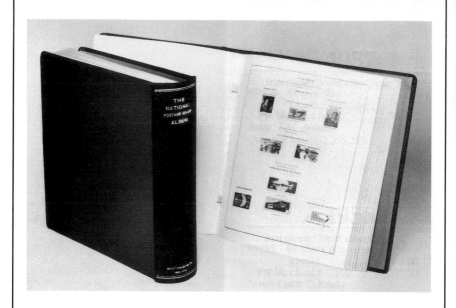

UNITED STATES

NATIONAL ALBUM

THE SCOTT UNITED STATES NATIONAL POSTAGE STAMP ALBUM is "The" Album demanded by serious collectors of United States material.

The SCOTT NATIONAL POSTAGE STAMP ALBUM provides spaces for commemoratives, definitives, air post, special delivery, registration, certified mail, postage due, parcel post, special handling, officials, newspapers, offices abroad, hunting permits, confederates and much more!

Available in U.S.A. and Canada from your favorite dealer, bookstore or stamp collecting accessory retailer or write:

FLORIDA NO. **4410** -10

Blue-winged Teal
$3.50

Expires June 30, 1990

WATERFOWL STAMP

FLORIDA NO. **3670** -08

Wood Duck
$3.50

Expires June 30, 1991

WATERFOWL STAMP

1989

11    $3.50   Blue-winged teal,
         single (from sheet of 10) .   6.00
         a. with tab 15.00
Artist: J. Byron Test

1990

12    $3.50   Wood ducks, single
         (from sheet of 10) 6.00
         a. with tab 15.00
Artist: Ben Test

Not required to hunt waterfowl.

1985

1     $5.50   Wood ducks (from
           sheet of 30) 13.00
Artist: Daniel Smith

1986

2     $5.50   Mallards (from sheet
           of 30) 11.00
Artist: Jim Killen

1987

3     $5.50   Canada Geese (from
           sheet of 30) 7.50
Artist: James Partee, Jr.

1988

4     $5.50   Ring-necked ducks
           (from sheet of 30) 7.50
Artist: Paul Bridgeford

Required to hunt ducks.

1989

5	$5.50	Duckling & golden retriever puppy (from sheet of 20)	7.50

Artist: R.J. McDonald

6	$5.50	Wood ducks (from sheet of 20)	7.50

IDAHO

Printed in sheets of 30

1987

1	$5.50 Cinnamon teal	25.00
	a. booklet single (from pane of 5), rouletted, with full tab	17.50

Artist: Robert Leslie

1988

2	$5.50 Green-winged teal ...	10.00
	a. booklet single (from pane of 5), rouletted, with full tab	10.00

Artist: Jim Killen

1989

3	$6.00 Blue-winged teal	8.00
	a. booklet single (from pane of 5), rouletted, with full tab	8.50

Artist: Daniel Smith

The following items, through those issued in 1972, are daily usage stamps. They were required for hunting duck or geese or pheasants in state-operated waterfowl areas. Each issue had the same design: a state map with the four corners showing a goose in flight, a beaver, a fish, and a tree. Year date and fee are overprinted in black. Stamps are approximately 34x40mm. The listings below specify if the stamp was valid for hunting duck or hunting geese and pheasants.

1953

A1 $2 orange and black, *blue* (duck) . . . .   —

1956

A2 $2 green and black, *dull yellow* (duck) . . . .   —

1957

A3 $2 orange and black, *green* (duck) . . . .   —

1958

A4 $2 green and black, *dull yellow* (duck) . . . .   —

1959

A5 $3 green and black, *dull yellow* (duck) . . . .   —

A6 $5 red and black, *green* (geese & pheasants) . . . . .   —

1960

A7 $3 orange and black, *green* (duck) . . . .   —

A8 $5 green and black, *dull yellow* (geese & pheasants) . . . .   —

1961

A9 $3 green and black, *dull yellow* (duck) . . . .   —

A10 $5 red and black, *green* (geese & pheasants) . . . . .   —

1962

A11 $3 green and black, *dull yellow* (duck) . . . . —

A12 $5 red and black, *green* (geese & pheasants) . . . . . —

1963

A13 $3 orange and black, *green* (duck) . . . . —

A14 $5 green and black, *dull yellow* (geese & pheasants) . . . . —

1964

A15 $3 green and black, *dull yellow* (duck) . . . . —

A16 $5 red and black, *green* (geese & pheasants) . . . . . —

1965

A17 $3 orange and black, *green* (duck) . . . . —

A18 $5 green and black, *dull yellow* (geese & pheasants) . . . . —

1966

A19 $3 green and black, *dull yellow* (duck) . . . .   —

A20 $5 brown and black, *green* (geese & pheasants) . . . . .   —

1967

A21 $3 orange and black, *green* (duck) . . . .   —

A22 $5 green and black, *bright yellow* (geese & pheasants) . . . .   —

1968

A23 $3 green and black, *yellow* (duck) . . . .   —

A24 $5 brown and black, *green* (geese & pheasants) . . . . .   —

1969

A25 $3 orange and black, *green* (duck) . . . .   —

A26 $5 brown and black, *green* (geese & pheasants) . . . . .   —

1970

A27 $3 green and black, *dull yellow* (duck) . . . . —

A28 $5 brown and black, *green* (geese & pheasants) . . . . . —

1971

A29 $5 green and black, *dull yellow* (geese & pheasants) . . . . —

1972

A30 $3 orange and black, *green* (duck) . . . . —

A31 $5 brown and black, *green* (geese & pheasants) . . . . . —

ILLINOIS

Daily usage stamps for hunting duck reportedly were not issued for the years 1954, 1955 and 1971.

1975

1     $5 Mallard (from sheet of 10) 775.00
Artist: Robert Eschenfeldt

1976

2     $5 Wood ducks (from sheet of 10) 400.00
Artist: Robert G. Larson

1977

3     $5 Canada goose (from sheet of 10) 225.00
Artist: Richard Lynch

1978

4     $5 Canvasbacks (from sheet of 10) 115.00
Artist: Everett Staffeldt

ILLINOIS

1979

5    $5 Pintail (from sheet of 10) 115.00
Artist: John Eggert

1980

6    $5 Green-winged teal
       (from sheet of 10) 115.00
Artist: Bart Kassabaum

1981

7    $5 Widgeon (from sheet of
       10) 115.00
       a. "Green-winged Teal"
          (error, serial numbers
          1-1774 only) *800.00*
Artist: Jim Trandel

1982

8    $5 Black ducks (from sheet
       of 10) 65.00
Artist: Art Sinden

51

ILLINOIS

1983

9    $5   Lesser scaup (from sheet of 10) 60.00

Artist: Bart Kassabaum

1984

10    $5   Blue-winged teal (from sheet of 10) 55.00

Artist: George Kieffer

1985

11    $5   Redheads, booklet single (from pane of 5) 25.00
          a. with full tab 30.00

Artist: Bart Kassabaum

1986

12    $5   Gadwalls, booklet single (from pane of 5) 12.00
          a. with full tab 14.00

Artist: Art Sinden

1987

13 $5 Buffleheads, booklet
     single (from pane of 5) . . 10.00
          a. with full tab 12.00
Artist: Bart Kassabaum

1988

14 $5 Common goldeneyes,
     booklet single (from
     pane of 5) 8.00
          a. with full tab 9.00
Artist: Arthur Sinden

1989

15 $5 Ring-necked ducks,
     booklet single (from
     pane of 5) 7.50
          a. with full tab 8.50
Artist: Charles Freeman

1990

16 $10 Lesser snow goose,
     booklet single (from
     pane of 5) 14.00
          a. with full tab 15.00
Artist: John Henson

1976

1   $5 Green-winged teal,
    booklet single (from
    pane of 4) 9.00
Artist: Sonny Bashore

1977

2   $5 Pintail, booklet single
    (from pane of 4) 8.00
Artist: Sonny Bashore

1978

3   $5 Canada geese, booklet
    single (from pane of 4) ..   8.00
Artist: Carl "Spike" Knuth

1979

4   $5 Canvasbacks, booklet
    single (from pane of 4) ..   8.00
Artist: Diane Pierce

1980

5    $5 Mallard ducklings,
     booklet single (from
     pane of 4) 8.00
Artist: Dean R. Barrick

1981

6    $5 Hooded mergansers,
     booklet single (from
     pane of 4) 8.00
Artist: Rodney Crossman

1982

7    $5 Blue-winged teal,
     booklet single (from
     pane of 4) 8.00
Artist: George Metz

1983

8    $5 Snow geese, booklet
     single (from pane of 4) ..   8.00
Artist: Keith Freeman

1984

9     $5 Redheads, booklet single
          (from pane of 4) 8.00
Artist: Lyn Briggs

1985

10    $5 Pintail, booklet single
          (from pane of 4) 8.00
Artist: Rick Pas

1986

11    $5 Wood Duck, booklet
          single (from pane of 2)
          with tab 10.00
Artist: Ronald J. Louque

1987

12    $5 Canvasbacks, booklet
          single (from pane of 2)
          with tab 10.00
Artist: Susan Bates

1988

13 $6.75 Redheads, booklet
single (from pane of 2)
with tab 12.00
Artist: Bruce Langton

1989

14 $6.75 Canada goose, booklet
single (from pane of 2)
with tab 12.00
Artist: Ann C. Dahoney

1990

15 $6.75 Blue-winged teal,
booklet single (from
pane of 2) with tab 12.00
Artist: Ken Bucklew

IOWA

1972

1     $1 Mallards, booklet single
        (from pane of 5) 200.00
Artist: Maynard Reece
Shown at 85% of original size

1973

2     $1 Pintails, booklet single
        (from pane of 10) 65.00
Artist: Thomas Murphy
Shown at 85% of original size

1974

3     $1 Gadwalls, booklet single
        (from pane of 10) 85.00
Artist: James Landenberger
Shown at 85% of original size

1975

4     $1 Canada geese, booklet
        single (from pane of 10) . 125.00
Artist: Mark Reece
Shown at 85% of original size

1976

5     $1 Canvasbacks, booklet
        single (from pane of 10)   15.00
Artist: Nick Klepinger
Shown at 85% of original size

1977

6    $1 Lesser scaup, booklet
single (from pane of 10) . 15.00
Artist: Maynard Reece
Shown at 85% of original size

1978

7    $1 Wood ducks, booklet
single (from pane of 10) . 65.00
Artist: Nick Klepinger
Shown at 85% of original size

1979

8    $5 Buffleheads, booklet
single (from pane of 10) . 425.00
Artist: Andrew Peters
Shown at 85% of original size

1980

9    $5 Redheads, booklet single
(from pane of 10) 67.50
Artist: Paul Bridgford
Shown at 85% of original size

1981

10    $5 Green-winged teal,
booklet single (from
pane of 10) 35.00
Artist: Brad Reece
Shown at 85% of original size

1982

11    $5 Snow geese, booklet
single (from pane of 10) .   15.00
Artist: Tom Walker
Shown at 85% of original size

1983

12    $5 Widgeon, booklet single
(from pane of 10) 15.00
Artist: Paul Bridgford
Shown at 85% of original size

1984

13    $5 Wood ducks, booklet
single (from pane of 10) .   30.00
Artist: Larry Zach
Shown at 85% of original size

1985

14    $5 Mallard & mallard decoy,
booklet single (from
pane of 10) 16.00
Artist: Jack C. Hahn
Shown at 85% of original size

1986

15    $5 Blue-winged teal,
booklet single (from
pane of 10) 16.00
Artist: Paul Bridgford
Shown at 85% of original size

1987

16   $5 Canada goose, booklet
       single (from pane of 10) . 11.00
Artist: John Heidersbach
Shown at 85% of original size

1988

17   $5 Pintails, booklet single
       (from pane of 10) 9.00
Artist: Mark Cary
Shown at 85% of original size

1989

18   $5 Blue-winged teal,
       booklet single (from
       pane of 10) 8.50
Artist: Jack Hohn
Shown at 85% of original size

1990

19   $5 Canvasback (from sheet
       of 10), serial numbers
       1-25,000 . . . . 8.00
      a. booklet single (from
        pane of 10), serial
        numbers 25,001-75,000 8.00
Artist: Patrick Murillo
Shown at 85% of original size

1987

1   \$3 Green-winged teal,
booklet single (from
pane of 10) 9.00
      a. serial number prefix
"DD" 9.00
      b. serial number prefix
"SS" 9.00

Artist: Guy Coheleach

1988

2   \$3 Canada geese (from sheet
of 30) 6.00
      a. booklet single (from
pane of 10) 8.00

Artist: Ann Dahoney

1989

3   \$3 Mallards (from sheet of
30) 6.00
      a. booket single (from
pane of 10) 8.00

Artist: Leon Parson

1985

1    $5.25 Mallards, booklet
single (from pane of 5)
with tab 9.00
Artist: Ray Harm

1986

2    $5.25 Wood ducks, booklet
single (from pane of 5)
with tab 8.50
Artist: Dave Chapple

1987

3    $5.25 Black ducks, booklet
single (from pane of 5)
with tab 8.50
Artist: R.J. McDonald

1988

4    $5.25 Canada goose, booklet
single (from pane of 5)
with tab 8.50
Artist: Lynn Kaatz

1989

5    $5.25 Canvasback, booklet
       single (from pane of 5)
       with tab 8.50
Artist: Philip Crowe

1990

6    $5.25 Widgeon, booklet
       single (from pane of 5)
       with tab 8.50
Artist: Jim Oliver

Printed in sheets of 30.

1989

1	$5 Blue-winged teal (resident)	8.00
2	$7.50 Blue-winged teal (non-resident)	10.00

Artist: David Noll

MAINE

Printed in sheets of 10.

1984

1	$2.50	Black ducks	30.00

Artist: David Maass

1985

2	$2.50	Common eiders	50.00

Artist: David Maass

1986

3	$2.50	Wood ducks	10.00

Artist: David Maass

1987

4	$2.50	Buffleheads	7.00

Artist: Ron Van Gilder

1988

5     $2.50 Green-winged teal ...   5.50
Artist: Rick Allen

1989

6     $2.50 Common goldeneyes .   5.00
Artist: Jeannine Staples

Printed in sheets of 10.

1974

1     $1.10   Mallards, with tab 25.00
Artist: John Taylor
Shown at 70% of original size

1975

2     $1.10   Canada geese, with
         tab 7.50
Artist: Stanley Stearns
Shown at 70% of original size

1976

3     $1.10   Canvasbacks, with tab   6.00
Artist: Louis Frisino
Shown at 70% of original size

1977

4     $1.10   Greater scaup, with
         tab 6.00
Artist: Jack Schroeder
Shown at 70% of original size

1978

5     $1.10   Redheads, with tab ...   6.00
Artist: Stanley Stearns
Shown at 70% of original size

1979

6     $1.10 Wood ducks, with tab   6.00
Artist: John Taylor
Shown at 70% of original size

1980

7     $1.10 Pintail decoy, with
            tab 6.00
Artist: Jack Schroeder
Shown at 70% of original size

1981

8     $3 Widgeon, with tab 6.00
Artist: Arthur R. Eakin
Shown at 70% of original size

1982

9     $3 Canvasback, with tab . . .   9.00
Artist: Roger Bucklin
Shown at 70% of original size

1983

10     $3 Wood duck, with tab 12.50
Artist: Roger Lent
Shown at 70% of original size

1984

11     $6 Black ducks, with tab . . .   8.50
Artist: Carla Huber
Shown at 70% of original size

1985

12   $6 Canada geese, with tab ..   8.00
Artist: David Turnbaugh
Shown at 70% of original size

1986

13   $6 Hooded mergansers, with tab 8.00
Artist: Louis Frisino
Shown at 70% of original size

1987

14   $6 Redheads, with tab 8.00
Artist: Francis E. Sweet
Shown at 70% of original size

1988

15   $6 Ruddy ducks, with tab ..   8.00
Artist: Christopher White
Shown at 70% of original size

1989

16   $6 Blue-winged teal, with tab 8.00
Artist: Roger E. Lent
Shown at 70% of original size

Printed in sheets of 12.

1974

1    $1.25 Wood duck decoy 12.00
Artist: Milton C. Weiler

1975

2    $1.25 Pintail decoy 10.00
Artist: Tom Hennessey

1976

3    $1.25 Canada goose decoy .. 10.00
Artist: William P. Tyner

1977

4    $1.25 Goldeneye decoy 10.00
Artist: William P. Tyner

1978 Massachusetts Waterfowl Stamp

Black Duck by A. Elmer Crowell $1.25

1979 Massachusetts Waterfowl Stamp

$1.25 Ruddy Turnstone by Lothrop Holmes

1980 Massachusetts Waterfowl Stamp

$1.25 Canvas and slat Oldsquaw by Lothrop Holmes

1981 Massachusetts Waterfowl Stamp

$1.25 Red-Breasted Merganser by an unknown carver

1978

| 5 | $1.25 | Black duck decoy | .... | 9.00 |

Artist: William P. Tyner

1979

| 6 | $1.25 | Ruddy duck decoy | ... | 9.00 |

Artist: Randy Julius

1980

| 7 | $1.25 | Old squaw decoy | .... | 7.50 |

Artist: John Eggert

1981

| 8 | $1.25 | Red-breasted merganser decoy | .... | 7.50 |

Artist: Randy Julius

1982

9 $1.25 Greater yellowlegs
        decoy 7.50
Artist: John Eggert

1983

10 $1.25 Redhead decoy 6.00
Artist: Randy Julius

1984

11 $1.25 White-winged scoter
        decoy 6.00
Artist: Joseph Cibula

1985

12 $1.25 Ruddy duck decoy ... 5.00
Artist: Randy Julius

1986

13    $1.25 Bluebill decoy 5.00
Artist: Robert Piscatori

1987

14    $1.25 Widgeon decoy 5.00
Artist: Peter Baedita

1988

15    $1.25 Mallard decoy 5.00
Artist: Bob Piscatori

1989

16    $1.25 Brant decoy 5.00
Artist: Lou Barnicle

$1.25 Massachusetts Waterfowl Stamp

Whistler Hen by C.H. Hart

1990

1990

| 17 | $1.25 Whistler hen goldeneye decoy .... | 3.00 |

Artist: Rachel Schreve

*Printed in sheets of 10
with center gutter, rouletted.*

1976

1    $2.10 Wood duck 10.00
Artist: Oscar Warbach

1977

2    $2.10 Canvasbacks 350.00
Artist: Larry Hayden

1978

3    $2.10 Mallards, with tab 45.00
Artist: Richard Timm
Shown at 85% of original size

1979

4    $2.10 Canada geese, with
               tab 55.00
Artist: Andrew Kurzmann
Shown at 85% of original size

MICHIGAN

1980

5    $3.75 Lesser scaup, with tab   25.00
Artist: Larry Hayden
Shown at 85% of original size

1981

6    $3.75 Buffleheads, self-
adhesive on wax backed
paper 25.00
Artist: Dietmar Krumrey

1982

7    $3.75 Redheads, self-
adhesive on wax-backed
paper 25.00
Artist: G. van Frankenhuyzen
Shown at 85% of original size

1983

8    $3.75 Wood ducks, self-
adhesive 27.50
Artist: Rod Lawrence
Shown at 85% of original size

MICHIGAN WATERFOWL

1984   **P 014864** $3.75

1985   **U 000303** $3.75

MICHIGAN WATERFOWL

Issued Mo. _____ Day _____

1986   **W 106683**

MICHIGAN WATERFOWL

Issued Mo. _____ Day _____

1984

9    $3.75   Pintails, self-adhesive   25.00
Artist: Larry Cory
Shown at 85% of original size

1985

10    $3.75   Ring-necked ducks,
              self-adhesive 20.00
Artist: Robert Steiner
Shown at 85% of original size

1986

11    $3.75   Common goldeneyes,
              self-adhesive 11.00
Artist: Russell Cobane
Shown at 85% of original size

1987

12   $3.85 Green-winged teal,
         self-adhesive 10.00
Artist: Larry Hayden
Shown at 85% of original size

1988

13   $3.85 Canada geese, self-
         adhesive 8.00
Artist: John Martens
Shown at 85% of original size

1989

14   $3.85 Widgeon, self-
         adhesive 6.00
Artist: Deitmar Krumrey
Shown at 85% of original size

Printed in sheets of 10.

1977

1    $3 Mallards 14.00
Artist: David Maass

1978

2    $3 Lesser scaup 5.00
Artist: Leslie C. Kouba

1979

3    $3 Pintails 5.00
Artist: David Maass

1980

4    $3 Canvasbacks 5.00
Artist: James Meger

1981

5      $3 Canada geese 5.00
Artist: Terry Redlin

1982

6      $3 Redheads 5.00
Artist: Phil Scholer

1983

7      $3 Blue geese & snow goose   5.00
Artist: Gary Moss

1984

8      $3 Wood ducks 5.00
Artist: Thomas Gross

1985

9    $3 White-fronted geese 5.00
Artist: Terry Redlin

1986

10    $5 Lesser scaup 7.50
Artist: Brian Jarvi

*Beginning with this issue, left side of
sheets have an agent's tab, detachable
from the numbered tab.*

1987

11    $5 common goldeneyes,
         with numbered tab 7.50
Artist: Ron Van Gilder

1988

12    $5 Buffleheads, with
         numbered tab 7.50
Artist: Robert Hautman

1989

13    $5 Widgeon, with
        numbered tab 7.50
Artist: Jim Hautman

1990

14    $5 Hooded mergansers,
        with numbered tab 7.50
Artist: Kevin Daniel

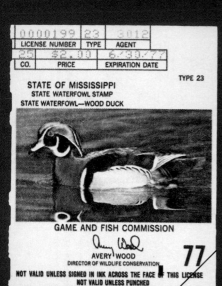

TYPE 23

STATE OF MISSISSIPPI
STATE WATERFOWL STAMP
STATE WATERFOWL—WOOD DUCK

GAME AND FISH COMMISSION

AVERY WOOD
DIRECTOR OF WILDLIFE CONSERVATION

77

NOT VALID UNLESS SIGNED IN INK ACROSS THE FACE OF THIS LICENSE
NOT VALID UNLESS PUNCHED

Stamps are rouletted.

1976

1	$2	Wood duck, part of data processing card	12.50
	a.	complete 2-part data processing card	16.00

Artists: Carroll & Gwen Perkins
Shown at 85% of original size

1977

2	$2	Mallards (from sheet of 10)	5.00

Artist: Allen Hughes

1978

3	$2	Green-winged teal (from sheet of 10)	5.00

Artist: John Reimers

1979

4	$2 Canvasbacks (from sheet of 10)	5.00

Artist: Carole Pigott Hardy

1980

5	$2 Pintails (from sheet of 10)	5.00

Artist: Bob Tompkins

1981

6	$2 Redheads (from sheet of 10)	5.00

Artist: John Reimers

1982

7	$2 Canada geese (from sheet of 10)	5.00

Artist: Jerry Johnson

1983

8    $2 Lesser scaup (from sheet
        of 10) 5.00
Artist: Jerrie Glasper

1984

9    $2 Black ducks (from sheet
        of 10) 5.00
Artist: Tommy Goodman

1985

10   $2 Mallards, horizontal
        serial number and silver
        bar (from sheet of 10) ...   5.00
        a. vertical serial number,
            imperf. between serial
            number and stamp 75.00
        b. horizontal serial num-
            ber & no vertical silver
            bar 275.00
Artist: Lottie Fulton

1986

11   $2 Widgeon (from sheet
        of 10) 5.00
Artist: Joe Latil

1987

| 12 | $2 Ring-necked ducks (from sheet of 10) . . . . | 5.00 |

Artist: Robert Garner

1988

| 13 | $2 Snow geese (from sheet of 10) . . . . | 4.00 |

Artist: Bob Tompkins

1989

| 14 | $2 Wood ducks (from sheet of 10) . . . . | 4.00 |

Artist: Debra Swartzendruber

1979

1    $3.40 Canada geese, booklet
single (from pane of 5),
rouletted *800.00*
    a. with tab . . . . *1000.*
Artist: Charles W. Schwartz

1980

2    $3.40 Wood ducks, booklet
single (from pane of 5),
rouletted 175.00
    a. with tab 250.00
Artist: David Plank

1981

3    $3 Lesser scaup, booklet
single (from pane of 5),
rouletted 85.00
    a. with tab 110.00
Artist: Tom Crain

1982

4    $3 Buffleheads, booklet
single (from pane of 5),
rouletted 50.00
    a. with tab 70.00
Artist: Gary Lucy

1983

5    $3 Blue-winged teal,
     booklet single (from
     pane of 5), rouletted 55.00
        a. with tab 80.00
Artist: Doug Ross

1984

6    $3 Mallards, booklet single
     (from pane of 5),
     rouletted 50.00
        a. with tab 70.00
Artist: Glenn Chambers

1985

7    $3 Widgeon, booklet single
     (from pane of 5),
     rouletted 25.00
        a. with tab 25.00
Artist: Ron Clayton

1986

8    $3 Hooded mergansers,
     booklet single (from
     pane of 5), rouletted 18.00
        a. with tab 22.50
Artist: Tom Crain

1987

9     $3 Pintails, booklet single
(from pane of 5),
rouletted 10.00
         a. with tab 12.50
Artist: Ron Ferkol

1988

10    $3 Canvasbacks, booklet
single (from pane of 5) . .   8.00
         a. with tab 10.00
Artist: Bruce Bollman

1989

11    $3 Ringnecks, booklet
single (from pane of 5) . .   5.00
         a. with tab 7.00
Artist: Kathy Dickson

Not required to hunt waterfowl.

1969

A1	$1 Sage grouse (children) ..	—
A2	$2 Sage grouse (resident) ...	—
A3	$25 Sage grouse (non-resident)	—

1970

A4	$1 Sage grouse (children) ..	—
A5	$2 Sage grouse (resident) ...	—
A6	$25 Sage grouse (non-resident)	—

1971

A7	$1 Pheasant (children)	—
A8	$2 Pheasant (resident)	—
A9	$25 Pheasant (non-resident)	—

1972

A10	$1	Pheasant (children)	—
A11	$2	Pheasant (resident)	—
A12	$25	Pheasant (non-resident)	—

1973

A13	$1	Pheasant (children)	—
A14	$2	Pheasant (resident)	—
A15	$25	Pheasant (non-resident)	—

1974

A16	$1	Pheasant (children)	—
A17	$2	Pheasant (resident)	—
A18	$25	Pheasant (non-resident)	—

1975

A19	$1 Pheasant (children)	—
A20	$2 Pheasant (resident)	—
A21	$25 Pheasant (non-resident)	—

1976

A22	$2 Pheasant (children)	—
A23	$4 Pheasant (resident)	—
A24	$30 Pheasant (non-resident)	—

1977

A25	$2 Pheasant (children)	—
A26	$4 Pheasant (resident)	—
A27	$30 Pheasant (non-resident)	—

1978

A28 $2 Sage grouse (from sheet of 10) (children) . . . .   —

A29 $4 Sage grouse (from sheet of 10) (resident) . . . .   —

A30 $30 Sage grouse (from sheet of 10) (non-resident) . . . .   —

1979

A31 $2 Snow geese (from sheet of 10) (children) . . . .   —

A32 $4 Snow geese (from sheet of 10) (resident) . . . .   —

A33 $30 Snow geese (from sheet of 10) (non-resident) . . . .   —

A non-denominated item showing a Goldeneye was not required for hunting and included the inscription "This Stamp Is Not a Hunting License."

Required for hunting waterfowl.

1986

1   $5 Canada geese (from sheet of 30) 17.50
- **a.** booklet horizontal pair with side tabs (from pane of 10) . . . . —
- **b.** booklet top pair with top and side tabs . . . . . —
- **c.** booklet bottom pair with bottom and side tabs . . . . —

Artist: Joe Thornbrugh

1987

2   $5 Redheads (from sheet of 30) 14.00
- **a.** booklet horizontal pair with side tabs (from pane of 10) 45.00
- **b.** booklet top pair with top and side tabs 80.00
- **c.** booklet bottom pair with bottom and side tabs 60.00

Artist: Roger Cruwys

1988

3    $5 Mallards (from sheet of
30) 10.00
    a. booklet horizontal pair
with side tabs (from
pane of 10) *25.00*
    b. booklet top pair with
top and side tabs *55.00*
    c. booklet bottom pair
with bottom and side
tabs *40.00*
Artist: Dave Samuelson

1989

4    $5 Black Labrador retriever
& pintail (from sheet
of 30) 8.00
    a. booklet horizontal pair
with side tabs (from
pane of 10) *20.00*
    b. booklet top pair with
top and side tabs *35.00*
    c. booklet bottom pair
with bottom and side
tabs *25.00*
Artist: Roger Cruwys

1990

5    $5 Blue-winged teal &
cinnamon teal 8.00
Artist: Joe Thronbrugh

Tabs must be cut from sheets of 4.

1979

1	$2 Canvasbacks & decoy	...	65.00
	a. with tab	....	75.00

Artist: Larry Hayden

1980

2	$2 Cinnamon teal	....	12.50
	a. with tab	....	15.00

Artist: Dick McRill

1981

3	$2 Whistling swan	....	11.00
	a. with tab	....	13.50

Artist: Phil Scholer

1982

4	$2 Shovelers	....	11.00
	a. with tab	....	13.50

Artist: Richard Timm
Shown at 85% of original size

1983

| 5 | $2 Gadwalls | 11.00 |
| | **a.** with tab | 13.50 |

Artist: Charles Allen
Shown at 85% of original size

1984

| 6 | $2 Pintails | 11.00 |
| | **a.** with tab | 13.50 |

Artist: Robert Steiner
Shown at 85% of original size

1985

| 7 | $2 Lesser Canada geese | 12.50 |
| | **a.** with tab | 15.00 |

Artist: Richard Wilson
Shown at 85% of original size

1986

| 8 | $2 Redheads | 12.50 |
| | **a.** with tab | 15.00 |

Artist: Nolan Haas
Shown at 85% of original size

1987

9	$2 Buffleheads	8.00
	a. with tab	10.00

Artist: Sherrie Russell
Shown at 85% of original size

1988

10	$2 Canvasbacks (second printing, serial numbers 30,001 and above)	8.00
	a. with tab (first printing, serial numbers 1-30,000)	10.00

Artist: Jim Hautman
Shown at 85% of original size

1989

11	$2 Ross's geese (serial numbers 1-50,000)	4.00
	a. with tab (serial numbers 50,001-75-000)	15.00

Artist: Robert Hautman
Shown at 85% of original size
Serial numbers on 1989 stamps from 50,001-75,000 were available only from Nevada hunter licensing agents.

DUCKS
AT
FACE!

- MINT NEVER HINGED -

Take advantage of this spectacular offer!
State Ducks at face value!

This special for readers of the Scott Catalogue is
unprecedented in its value to collectors. Perfect for new
collectors or as a complement to an existing collection!

All Stamps Mint, VF, OG, NH.

★ GROUP 1 ★	★ GROUP 2 ★	★ GROUP 3* ★
10 Different	15 Different	25 DIFF. *Includes a 1976 First of state.
$35.50	$52.50	$78.15

ORDER TOLL-FREE 800-231-5926
Please - no dealer orders.

Sam Houston Duck Company

P.O. Box 820087, Dept. B
Houston, TX 77282

From sheets of 30.

1983

1    $4 Wood ducks 175.00
      a. booklet single, with
          full (3-part) tab 275.00
Artist: Richard Plasschaert

1984

2    $4 Mallards 140.00
      a. booklet single, with
          full (3-part) tab 180.00
Artist: Phillip Crowe

1985

3    $4 Blue-winged teal 125.00
      a. booklet single, with
          full (3-part) tab 135.00
Artist: Tom Hirata

1986

4    $4 Hooded mergansers 25.00
      a. booklet single, with
          full (3-part) tab 35.00
Artist: Durrant Ball

NEW HAMPSHIRE

1987

5	$4 Canada geese		10.00
	a. booklet single, with full (3-part) tab		16.00

Artist: Robert Steiner

1988

6	$4 Buffleheads		8.00
	a. booklet single, with full (3-part) tab		10.00

Artist: Robert Steiner

1989

7	$4 Black ducks		6.50
	a. booklet single, with full (3-part) tab		8.00

Artist: Robert Steiner

Printed from sheets of 30.

1984

1	$2.50 Canvasbacks (resident)	50.00
	a. booklet single (from pane of 10)	75.00
2	$5 Canvasbacks (non-resident)	65.00

Artist: Tom Hirata

1985

3	$2.50 Mallards (resident) . . .	20.00
	a. booklet single (from pane of 10) (serial numbers 50,000-)	35.00
4	$5 Mallards (non-resident) .	25.00

Artist: David Maass

1986

5	$2.50 Pintails (resident)	10.00
	a. booklet single (from pane of 10) (serial numbers 50,000-)	15.00
6	$5 Pintails (non-resident) . . .	20.00

Artist: Ronald J. Louque

1987

7	$2.50 Canada geese (resident)	7.00
	a. booklet single (from pane of 10)	9.00
8	$5 Canada geese (non-resident)	12.00
	a. booklet single (from pane of 10)	15.00

Artist: Louis Frisine

1988

9    $2.50 Green-winged teal
(resident) 5.00
      a. booklet single (from
         pane of 10) 6.00

10    $5 Green-winged teal
(non-resident) 10.00
      a. booklet single (from
         pane of 10) 11.00

Artist: Robert Leslie

1989

11    $2.50 Snow geese (resident)   5.00
      a. booklet single (from
         pane of 10) 6.00

12    $5 Snow geese
(non-resident) 10.00
      a. booklet single (from
         pane of 10) 11.00

Artist: Daniel Smith

Not required to hunt. Printed in sheets of 30.

1985

1 $5.50 Canada geese 15.00
Artist: Larry Barton

1986

2 $5.50 Mallards 12.00
Artist: David Maass

1987

3 $5.50 Wood ducks 11.00
Artist: Lee LeBlanc

1988

4 $5.50 Pintails 8.00
Artist: Richard Plasschaert

1989

5     $5.50   Greater Scaup 8.00
Artist: Robert Bateman

Not required to hunt until 1988.
Printed in sheets of 30.

1983

1    $5.50 Mallards 100.00
Artist: Richard Plasschaert

1984

2    $5.50 Wood ducks 65.00
Artist: Jim Killen

1985

3    $5.50 Canvasbacks 40.00
Artist: Tom Hirata

1986

4    $5.50 Canada geese 15.00
Artist: Tom Hirata

1987

5     $5.50 Pintails 12.00
Artist: Larry Barton

Required to hunt duck.

1988

6     $5 Green-winged teal 10.00
Artist: Ronald J. Louque

1989

7     $5 Snow geese 8.00
Artist: Louis Frisino

1990

8     $5 Redheads 8.00
Artist: Robert Leslie

17	18	19	20	21	22	23	24	25	26	27	28	29	30	31

☐ SEPT. 1975 - Zone _____ $5   1975
☐ OCT.   State of N. Dak.
         NR. Waterfowl Stamp
☐ NOV.   NON-TRANSFERABLE
☐ DEC.   N. Dak. Game & Fish Dept.

1	2	3	4	5	6	7	8	9	10	11	12	13	14	15	16

1975

A1 $5 green (self-adhesive with backing paper, die cut) . . —
Shown at 70% of original size

17	18	19	20	21	22	23	24	25	26	27	28	29	30	31

☐ SEPT. 1976 - Zone _____ $5   1976
☐ OCT.   State of N. Dak.
         NR. Waterfowl Stamp N⁰   6356
☐ NOV.   NON-TRANSFERABLE
☐ DEC.   N. Dak. Game & Fish Dept.

1	2	3	4	5	6	7	8	9	10	11	12	13	14	15	16

1976

A2 $5 red and black (self-adhesive with backing paper, die cut) . . . . —
Shown at 70% of original size

17	18	19	20	21	22	23	24	25	26	27	28	29	30	31

☐ SEPT. 1977 - Zone _____ $5   1977
☐ OCT.   State of N. Dak.
         NR. Waterfowl Stamp N⁰   5908
☐ NOV.   NON-TRANSFERABLE
☐ DEC.   N. Dak. Game & Fish Dept.

1	2	3	4	5	6	7	8	9	10	11	12	13	14	15	16

1977

A3 $5 red (self-adhesive with backing paper, die cut) . . —
Shown at 70% of original size

N. Dak. Game & Fish Dept.
☐ SEPT. 1978 - Zone _____ $5   1978
☐ OCT.   State of N.Dak.
         NR. Waterfowl N⁰   9391
☐ NOV.   Stamp
☐ DEC.   NON-TRANSFERABLE

1	2	3	4	5	6	7	8	9	10	11	12	13	14	15	16
17	18	19	20	21	22	23	24	25	26	27	28	29	30	31	

1978

A4 $5 red and black (self-adhesive with backing paper, die cut) . . . . —
Shown at 70% of original size

N. Dak. Game & Fish Dept.
☐ SEPT. 1979 - Zone _____ $5   1979
☐ OCT.   State of N.Dak.
☐ NOV.   NR. Waterfowl N⁰   5739
         Stamp
☐ DEC.   NON-TRANSFERABLE

1	2	3	4	5	6	7	8	9	10	11	12	13	14	15	16
17	18	19	20	21	22	23	24	25	26	27	28	29	30	31	

1979

A5 $5 red (self-adhesive with backing paper, die cut) . . —
Shown at 70% of original size

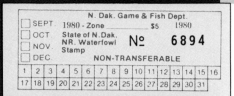

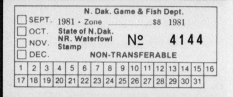

1980

A6 $5 green (self-adhesive with backing paper, die cut) ..   ——
Shown at 70% of original size

1981

A7 $5 blue and black (self-adhesive with backing paper, die cut) ....   ——
Shown at 70% of original size

The above stamps all were required for use by non-residents hunting waterfowl.

The stamps that follow are noted for use by residents or non-residents. All non-resident stamps are non-pictorial (text) only.

1982

A8 $8 black, self-adhesive with backing paper, die cut (non-resident) ....   ——
Shown at 70% of original size

1   $9 Canada geese (sheet of 30) (resident) (serial numbers 150,001-) 150.00
    a. booklet single (from pane of 5), with selvage on both sides (serial numbers 20,001-150,000) .... ——
    b. sheet stamp, serial numbers 1-20,000 (sheet of 10) .... ——
Artist: Richard Plasschaert

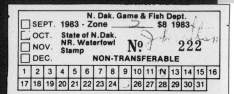

1983

A9 $8 black, self-adhesive with
backing paper, die cut
(non-resident) .... —
Shown at 70% of original size

2 $9 Mallards (from sheet of
30) (resident) 80.00
   a. booklet single (from
pane of 5), with sel-
vage on both sides
(serial numbers 20,001-
150,000) .... —
   b. Missing "No." and
larger serial number .. 160.00
Artist: Terry Redlin

1984

A10 $8 black, self-adhesive with
backing paper, die cut
(non-resident) .... —
Shown at 70% of original size

3 $9 Canvasbacks (from sheet
of 30) (resident) 30.00
   a. booklet single (from
pane of 5, serial num-
bers 20,001-150,000) ... —
Artist: David Maass

1985

A11 $8 black, rouletted (non-
resident) . . . . —
Shown at 60% of original size

4 $9 Bluebills (from sheet of
30) (resident) 25.00
    a. booklet single (from
    pane of 5, serial num-
    bers 20,001-150,000) . . . —
Artist: Leslie C. Kouba

1986

A12 $8 black, rouletted, with
serial number, small
characters (non-resident) —
    a. no serial number, large
    characters . . . . —
Shown at 60% of original size

5 $9 Pintails (from sheet of
30) (resident) 16.00
    a. booklet single (from
    pane of 5, serial num-
    bers 20,001-150,000) . . . *600.00*
Artist: Mario Fernandez

1987

A13 $8 black, rouletted (non-resident) . . . . —
Shown at 60% of original size

6    $9 Snow geese (from sheet
          of 30) (resident) 14.00
      a. booklet single (from
          pane of 5, serial num-
          bers 20,001-140,000) . . . 70.00
Artist: Ronald J. Louque

1988

A14 $8 black, rouletted (non-resident) . . . . —
Shown at 60% of original size

7    $9 White-winged scoters
          (from sheet of 30)
          (resident) 12.50
      a. booklet single (from
          pane of 5, serial num-
          bers 20,001-140,000) . . . 25.00
Artist: Louis Frisino

1989

8	$6 Redheads (from sheet of 30) (resident)	9.00
	a. booklet single (from pane of 5, serial numbers 20,001-140,000) ...	12.50

Artist: Robert Leslie

A15	$8 black, *green*, rouletted (non-resident)	—

Shown at 60% of original size

1990

9	$6 Mallard	9.00

Artist: Roger Cruwys

Printed in sheets of 16, of which eight stamps in the sheet are attached to selvage with numbers.

1982

1     $5.75 Wood ducks 95.00
Artist: John A. Ruthven

1983

2     $5.75 Mallards 85.00
Artist: Harry Antis

1984

3     $5.75 Green-winged teal . . .   80.00
Artist: Harold Roe

1985

4     $5.75 Redheads 60.00
Artist: Ronald J. Louque

1986

5     $5.75 Canvasback 16.00
Artist: Lynn Kaatz

1987

6     $6 Blue-winged teal 12.00
Artist: Harold Roe

1988

7     $6 Common goldeneyes 9.00
Artist: Cynthia Fisher

1989

8     $6 Canada geese 8.00
Artist: Lynn Kaatz

1990

11    $9 Black ducks 14.00
Artist: Jon Henson

OKLAHOMA

1980

1     $4 Pintails, booklet single
(from pane of 10) 45.00
Artist: Pat Sawyer

1981

2     $4 Canada goose, booklet
single (from pane of 10) .   40.00
Artist: Hoyt Smith

1982

3     $4 Green-winged teal,
booklet single (from
pane of 10) 12.00
Artist: Jeffrey Frey

1983

4     $4 Wood ducks, booklet
single (pane of 5)
with full tab 8.00
Artist: Gerald Mobley

1984

5   $4 Ring-necked ducks, booklet single (from pane of 5) with full tab ..   8.00
Artist: Hoyt Smith

1985

6   $4 Mallards, booklet single (from pane of 5) with full tab 8.00
Artist: Gerald Mobley

1986

7   $4 Snow geese, booklet single (from pane of 5) with full tab 8.00
Artist: Hoyt Smith

1987

8   $4 Canvasbacks, booklet single (from pane of 5) with full tab 8.00
Artist: Rayburn T. Foster

1988

9    $4 Widgeon, booklet single
(from pane of 5) with full
tab and serial numbers
31,001-40,000 . . . . *20.00*
     a. booklet single (from pane
of 5) with full tab and
serial numbers 1- 30,000   7.00
Artist: Jim Gaar

1989

10    $4 Redheads (from sheet of
30) 8.00
     a. booklet single (from
pane of 5) with full tab
and serial numbers 1-
30,000 . . . .   9.00
Artist: Wanda Mumm

1984 Oregon Waterfowl Stamp

1985 Oregon Waterfowl Stamp

1986 Oregon Waterfowl Stamp

1987 Oregon Waterfowl Stamp

1984

1    $5 Canada geese (from sheet of 30) 40.00
Artist: Michael Sieve

1985

2    $5 Lesser snow geese (from sheet of 30) 55.00
     a. booklet single (from pane of 5) with full (3-part) tab 550.00
Artist: Michael Sieve

1986

3    $5 Pacific brant (from sheet of 30) 17.50
     a. booklet single (from pane of 5) with full (3-part) tab 30.00
Artist: Michael Sieve

1987

4    $5 White-fronted geese (from sheet of 30) 12.00
     a. booklet single (from pane of 5) with full (3-part) tab 16.00
Artist: D.M. Smith

1988 Oregon Waterfowl Stamp

1988

5    $5 Great Basin Canada geese
       (from sheet of 30) 9.00
       a. miniature sheet of 1 . . .   14.00
Artist: Darrell Davis

1989

6   Provisional issue, black
      serial numbers (001-
      16,000) 25.00
      a. red serial numbers
           (16,000-), could be
           used in 1990 and
           beyond 12.50
Shown at 70% of original size

1989 Oregon Waterfowl Stamp

7    $5 Black Labrador retriever
       & pintails (from sheet
       of 30) 8.00
       a. miniature sheet of 1 . . .   10.00
Artist: Philip Crowe

Issued in sheets of 10. Not required to hunt.

1983

1   $5.50 Wood ducks 40.00
Artist: Ned Smith

1984

2   $5.50 Canada geese 25.00
Artist: Jim Killen

1985

3   $5.50 Mallards 12.00
Artist: Ned Smith

1986

4   $5.50 Blue-winged teal 8.00
Artist: Robert C. Knutson

1987

5     $5.50   Pintails 8.00
Artist: Robert Leslie

1988

6     $5.50   Wood ducks 8.00
Artist: John Heldersbach

1989

7     $5.50   Hooded merganser . . .   8.00
Artist: Ronald J. Louque

1990

8     $5.50   Canvasbacks 8.00
Artist: Tom Hirata

RHODE ISLAND

1989

1	$7.50	Canvasbacks (from sheet of 30)	10.00
	a.	booklet single (from pane of 5) with full tab	12.00

Artist: Robert Steiner

Issued in sheets of 30.

1981

1    $5.50 Wood ducks 100.00
Artist: Lee LeBlanc

1982

2    $5.50 Mallards 100.00
        a. serial number on re-
           verse (selvage removed
           right and left of sheet
           before issue) *450.00*
Artist: Bob Binks

1983

3    $5.50 Pintails 120.00
        a. serial number on re-
           verse (selvage removed
           right and left of sheet
           before issue) *250.00*
Artist: Jim Killen

1984

4    $5.50 Canada geese 75.00
        a. serial number on re-
           verse (selvage removed
           right and left of sheet
           before issue) *200.00*
Artist: Al Dornisch

SOUTH CAROLINA

1985

5	$5.50 Green-winged teal ...	75.00
	a. serial number on reverse (selvage removed right and left of sheet before issue)	95.00

Artist: Rosemary Millette

1986

6	$5.50 Canvasbacks	25.00
	a. serial number on reverse (selvage removed right and left of sheet before issue)	40.00

Artist: Daniel Smith

1987

7	$5.50 Black ducks	15.00
	a. serial number on reverse (selvage removed right and left of sheet before issue)	17.50

Artist: Steve Dillard

1988

8	$5.50 Widgeon & spaniel ...	12.50
	a. serial number on reverse (selvage removed right and left of sheet before issue)	12.50

Artist: Jim Killen

1989

9	$5.50 Blue-winged teal	9.00

a. serial number on reverse (selvage removed right and left of sheet before issue) 9.00

Artist: Lee Cable

1990

10	$5.50 Wood ducks	9.00

a. serial number on reverse (selvage removed right and left of sheet before issue) 9.00

Artist: John Wilson

1949

A1 $1 black and green, red
serial number (text only)   ——

1950

A2 $1 black and brown, red
serial number, *yellow*
(text only) . . . .   ——

1970

A3 $30 black and red, *pink,*
booklet single (from
pane of 5) (non-resident)   ——
   a. missing serial number .   ——
Shown at 70% of original size

1971

A4 $30 black and red, *pink,*
booklet single (from
pane of 5) (non-resident)   ——
Shown at 70% of original size

1972

A5 $30 black and red, booklet
single (from pane of 5)
(non-resident) .... —
Shown at 70% of original size

1973

A6 $30 black and red, *blue,*
booklet single (from
pane of 5) (non-resident) —
Shown at 70% of original size

1974

A7 $30 black and red, *green,*
booklet single (from
pane of 5) (non-resident) —
    a. overprinted "1" ...... —
    b. overprinted "2" ...... —
    c. overprinted "4" ...... —
Shown at 70% of original size

1975

A8 $30 black and red, *yellow,*
booklet single (from
pane of 5) (non-resident) —
    a. overprinted "UNIT 1" . —
    b. overprinted "UNIT 2" . —
Shown at 70% of original size

1976

1	$1 Mallards, booklet single (from pane of 5), serial number 5mm high	20.00
	a. serial number 4mm high	*25.00*

Artist: Robert Kusserow

A9	$30 black and red, *yellow,* booklet single (from pane of 5), serial number 5mm high (non-resident)	—
	a. serial number 4mm high	—
	b. overprinted "1"	—
	c. overprinted "2"	—

Shown at 70% of original size

1977

2	$1 Pintails, booklet single (from pane of 5)	13.00

Artist: Don Steinbeck

A10	$30 black, *red,* booklet single (from pane of 5) (non-resident)	—
	a. overprinted "1"	—
	b. overprinted "2"	—
	c. overprinted "3"	—
	d. overprinted "4"	—
	e. overprinted "5"	—
	f. missing "7" in left year date	—

Shown at 70% of original size

1978

3    $1 Canvasbacks, booklet
single (from pane of 5) ..   9.00
Artist: John Moisan

A11 $30 black and red, *yellow,*
booklet single (from
pane of 5) (non-resident)   ——
Shown at 70% of original size

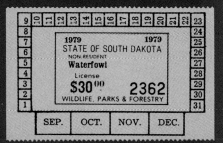

1979

A12 $30 black, *red,* booklet
single (from pane of 5)
(non-resident) ....   ——
Shown at 70% of original size

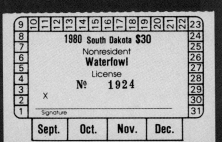

1980

A13 $30 black, *dull yellow,*
booklet single (from
pane of 5) (non-resident)   ——
      a. overprinted "1" ......   ——
Shown at 70% of original size

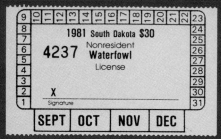

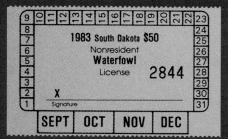

1981

A14 $30 black, *yellow,* booklet
single (from pane of 5)
(non-resident) . . . . —
    a. overprinted "UNIT 1" . —
Shown at 70% of original size

1982

A15 $30 black, *blue,* booklet
single (from pane of 5)
(non-resident) . . . . —
Shown at 70% of original size

A16 $50 black, *yellow,* booklet
single (from pane of 5)
(non-resident) . . . . —

1983

A17 $50 black, *red,* booklet
single (from pane of 5),
serial number in sans-
serif type (non-resident) . —
    a. serial number in serif
    type . . . . —
    b. overprinted "AREA 1" . —
    c. as "a," overprinted
    "AREA 1" . . . . —
    d. overprinted "AREA 2" . —
    e. as "a," overprinted
    "AREA 2" . . . . —
Shown at 70% of original size

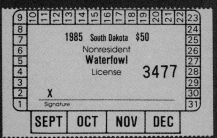

1984

A18 $50 black, *dull yellow,* booklet single (from pane of 5) (non-resident) ——
    a. overprinted "A" ...... ——
    b. overprinted "B" ...... ——
Shown at 70% of original size

1985

A19 $50 black, *red,* booklet single (from pane of 5) (non-resident) .... ——
Shown at 70% of original size

1986

4    $2 Canada Geese, booklet single (from pane of 5) .. 15.00
Artist: John Wilson

A20 $50 black, booklet single (from pane of 5) (non-resident) .... ——
Shown at 70% of original size

Beginning in 1987, South Dakota changed from a text-type non-resident stamp to a license.

1987

5    $2 Blue geese, booklet
        single (from pane of 5) ..   9.00
Artist: Rosemary Millette

1988

6    $2 White-fronted geese,
        booklet single (from
        pane of 5) 5.00
Artist: Marion Toillion

1989

7    $2 Mallards, booklet single
        (from pane of 5) 4.00
Artist: Rosemary Millette

1990

8    $2 Blue-winged teal,
        booklet single (from
        pane of 5) 4.00
Artist: John Green

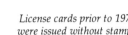

*License cards prior to 1979
were issued without stamps.*

1979

1    $2.30   Mallards, 1-part card
         (resident) 225.00
Shown at 85% of original size

2    $5.30   Mallards, 1-part card
         (non-resident)   . . . .   1250.
Artist: Dick Elliott

1980

3    $2.30   Canvasbacks, 1-part
         card (resident) 50.00
       a. single as full 3-part
         card 500.00
Shown at 85% of original size

4    $5.30   Canvasbacks, 1-part
         card (non-resident) 650.00
Artist: Phillip Crowe

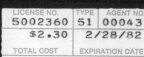

1981

5    $2.30 Wood ducks, 1-part
card 40.00
     a. single as full 3-part
card .... —

Artist: Bob Gillespie
Shown at 85% of original size

1982

6    $6.50 Canada geese, 1-part
card 75.00
     a. single as full 3-part
card .... —

Artist: Ken Schulz
Shown at 85% of original size

LICENSE NO.	TYPE	AGENT NO.	TYPE 05
5001963	05	00001	RESIDENT WATERFOWL LICENSE SUPPLEMENTAL TO COMBINATION HUNTING AND FISHING LICENSE
LIC. COST	FEE	TOTAL COST	
6.00	.50	6.50	
EXPIRATION DATE			
2/29/84			

TENNESSEE WILDLIFE RESOURCES AGENCY
MIGRATORY WATERFOWL STAMP
01963
PINTAILS
EXPIRES FEBRUARY 29, 1984 RESIDEN $6.00
83-84
SIGNATURE OF LICENSEE

LICENSE NO.	TYPE	AGENT NO.	TYPE 05
5002256	05	00001	RESIDENT WATERFOWL LICENSE SUPPLEMENTAL TO COMBINATION HUNTING AND FISHING LICENSE
LIC. COST	FEE	TOTAL COST	
6.00	.50	6.50	
EXPIRATION DATE			
2/28/85			

TENNESSEE WILDLIFE RESOURCES AGENCY
MIGRATORY WATERFOWL STAMP
02256
BLACK DUCK
EXPIRES FEBRUARY 28, 1985 RESIDE $6.00
84-85
SIGNATURE OF LICENSEE

1983

7   $6.50 Pintails, 1-part card .. 70.00
    a. single as full 3-part
        card 100.00
Artist: Phillip Crowe
Shown at 85% of original size

1984

8   $6.50 Black ducks, 1-part
        card 115.00
    a. single as full 3-part
        card 150.00
Artist: Allen Hughes
Shown at 85% of original size

1985

9   $6.50 Blue-winged teal,
      1-part card 30.00
        a. single as full 3-part
          card 75.00
Artist: Jimmy Stewart
Shown at 85% of original size

1986

10   $6.50 Mallard, 1-part card . .   20.00
        a. same, without printing   22.50
        b. single as full 3-part
          card 60.00
        c. same, without printing   60.00
        d. same, without printing
          and with inverted seri-
          al number 100.00
Artist: Ralph McDonald
Shown at 85% of original size

1987

11	$6.50 Canada geese, 1-part card	14.00
	a. same, without printing	14.00
	b. single as full 3-part card	15.00
	c. same, without printing	15.00
	d. expiration date "2/28/88"	—

Artist: Tom Hirata
Shown at 85% of original size
Computer printing on cards late in the issue year show a type style noticably different (letters are taller) than the earlier cards. These sell at a premium.

1988

12	$6.50 Canvasbacks, 1-part card	10.00
	a. single as 3-part card ...	15.00
	b. same, without printing	15.00
	c. single as full 4-part card	17.50
	d. same, without printing	17.50

Artist: Jim Lamb
Shown at 85% of original size

1989

13	$6.50	Green-winged teal, 1-part card	9.00
		a. single as 3-part card . . .	14.00
		b. same, without printing	14.00
		c. single as full 4-part card	15.00
		d. same, without printing	15.00

Artist: Roger Cruwys
Shown at 85% of original size

Printed in sheets of 10.

1981

1    $5 Mallards 70.00
Artist: Larry Hayden
Shown at 85% of original size

1982

2    $5 Pintails 50.00
Artist: Ken Carlson
Shown at 85% of original size

1983

3    $5 Widgeon 250.00
Artist: Maynard Reece
Shown at 85% of original size

1984

4    $5 Wood ducks 20.00
Artist: David Maass
Shown at 85% of original size

TEXAS

1985

5      $5 Snow geese 15.00
Artist: John Cowan
Shown at 85% of original size

1986

6      $5 Green-winged teal 12.00
Artist: Herb Booth
Shown at 85% of original size

1987

7      $5 White-fronted geese 10.00
Artist: Gary Moss
Shown at 85% of original size

1988

8      $5 Pintails 8.00
Artist: John Cowan
Shown at 85% of original size

TEXAS

1989

9    $5 Mallards 8.00
Artist: David Maass
Shown at 85% of original size

FIRST OF STATE **1986** Exp. 6-30-87

Printed in sheets of 30.

1986

1   $3.30 Whistling swans 12.00
Artist: Leon Parsons

1987

2   $3.30 Pintails 8.00
Artist: Arthur S. Anderson

1988

3   $3.30 Mallards 7.00
Artist: Dave Chapple

1989

4   $3.30 Canada geese 5.00
Artist: Jim Morgan

VERMONT

Printed in sheets of 30.

1986

1    $5 Wood ducks 14.00
Artist: Jim Killen

1987

2    $5 Common goldeneyes 11.00
Artist: Jim Killen

1988

3    $5 Black ducks 9.00
Artist: Jim Killen

1989

4    $5 Canada geese 7.00
Artist: Jim Killen

Not required to hunt. Printed in sheets of 30.

1988

1	$5	Mallards (serial numbers 1-40,020)	12.50
		a. booklet single (from pane of 10), serial numbers 40,021-70,000	12.50

Artist: Ronald J. Louque

1989

2	$5	Canada geese (serial numbers 1-40,020)	8.00
		a. booklet single (from pane of 10), serial numbers 40,021-70,000	9.00

Artist: Art LeMay

1986 Washington Waterfowl Stamp

Printed in sheets of 30.

1986

1	$5 Mallards (serial numbers 1-60,000)	....	15.00
	a. miniature sheet of 1 (serial numbers 60,001-160,000) from booklets of 25	....	35.00

Artist: Keith Warrick

1987

2	$5 Canvasbacks (serial numbers 1-24,000)	......	12.50
	a. miniature sheet of 1 (serial numbers 24,001-124,000) from booklets of 25	....	20.00

Artist: Ray Nichol

1988

3	$5 Harlequin (serial numbers 1-60,000)	......	9.00
	a. miniature sheet of 1 (serial numbers 60,001-160,000) from booklets of 25	....	12.00

Artist: Robert Bateman

1989

4	$5 Widgeon (serial numbers 1-60,000)	....	9.00
	a. miniature sheet of 1 (serial numbers 60,001-160,000) from booklets of 25	....	12.00

Artist: Maynard Reece

Printed in sheets of 30.

1987

1	$5 Canada geese ("RESIDENT")	15.00
	a. booklet single (from pane of 5)	40.00
2	$5 Canada geese ("NONRESIDENT")	15.00
	a. booklet single (from pane of 5)	40.00

Artist: Daniel Smith

1988

3	$5 waterfowl stamp certificate coupon	*175.00*
4	$5 Wood ducks ("RESIDENT")	10.00
	a. booklet single (from pane of 5)	15.00
	b. booklet single, serial numbers (45,001-50,000) on reverse	*75.00*
5	$5 Wood ducks ("NONRESIDENT")	10.00
	a. booklet single (from pane of 5)	15.00
	b. booklet single, serial numbers (53,001-58,000) on reverse	*75.00*

Artist: Steven Dillard

1989

6	$5 Decoys ("RESIDENT") ..	8.00
	a. booklet single (from pane of 5)	8.00
7	$5 Decoys ("NONRESIDENT")	8.00
	a. booklet single (from pane of 5)	8.00

Artist: Ronald J. Louque

1990

8	$5 Labrador retriever & decoy ("RESIDENT")	8.00
	a. booklet single (from pane of 5)	8.00
	b. booklet pane of 5	45.00
9	$5 Labrador retriever & decoy ("NONRESIDENT")......	8.00
	a. booklet single (from pane of 5)	8.00

Artist: Louis Frisino

Left side of sheet has an "agent tab," detachable from numbered tab, which is not normally collected from 1980 onward.

1978

| 1 | $3.25 | Wood ducks (from sheet of 10) . . . . | 150.00 |

Artist: Owen Gromme

1979

| 2 | $3.25 | Buffleheads (from sheet of 10) . . . . | 45.00 |

Artist: Carl "Spike" Knuth

1980

| 3 | $3.25 | Widgeon (from sheet of 10 with tab) . . . . | 15.00 |

Artist: Martin R. Murk

1981

| 4 | $3.25 | Lesser Scaup (from sheet of 10 with tab) . . . . | 15.00 |

Artist: Timothy C. Schultz

1982

5     $3.25 Pintails (from sheet of
        10 with tab) 8.00
Artist: William Koelpin

1983

6     $3.25 Blue-winged teal
        (from sheet of 10 with . . .
        tab) 8.00
Artist: Carl "Spike" Knuth

1984

7     $3.25 Hooded merganser
        (from sheet of 10 with
        tab) 8.00
Artist: Michael Riddet

1985

8     $3.25 Lesser Scaup (from
        sheet of 10 with tab) 10.00
Artist: Greg Alexander

WISCONSIN

1986

9    $3.25 Canvasbacks (from sheet of 10 with tab) 10.00
Artist: Don Moore

1987

10   $3.25 Canada geese (from sheet of 10 with tab) 6.00
Artist: Al Kraayvanger

1988

11   $3.25 Hooded merganser (from sheet of 10 with tab) 6.00
Artist: Richard Timm

1989

12   $3.25 Common goldeneye (from sheet of 10 with tab) 6.00
Artist: Rich Kelly

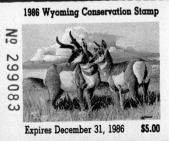

Issued in panes of 5. Required to fish as well as to hunt all small and big game. Proceeds from the sale of these stamps do not solely benefit waterfowl preservation.

1984

1	$5 Mockingbird	. . . .	8.00

1985

2	$5 Canada geese	. . . .	8.00

Artist: Robert Kusserow

1986

3	$5 Antelope	. . . .	8.00

1987

4    $5 Grouse 8.00

1988

5    $5 Fish 8.00

1989

6    $5 Deer 8.00

1990

7    $5 Bear 8.00

OTHER GOVERNMENTAL ISSUES

Following is a listing of permit stamps issued by governmental agencies for other than nationwide or statewide use. The items noted here were required for hunting waterfowl at specific areas.

CALIFORNIA

Required to hunt waterfowl on Honey Lake. Valid for a full season. Stamp design consists totally of text. The stamps are rouletted 9½.

1956-57

1	$5 black	....	—

1957-58

2	$5 black, *blue green*	....	—

1958-59

3	$5 black, *deep yellow*	....	—

Fee $5.00   220 H

STATE OF CALIFORNIA
DEPARTMENT OF FISH AND GAME
SEASONAL PERMIT for
HONEY LAKE
Valid during 1956-57 Waterfowl Season

Stamp must be pasted on back of
1956-57 Hunting License. Owner must
validate by signing name across face
of Stamp.   41214 8-56   SPO

Fee $5.00   75

STATE OF CALIFORNIA
DEPARTMENT OF FISH AND GAME
SEASONAL PERMIT for
HONEY LAKE
Valid during 1957-58 Waterfowl Season

Stamp must be pasted on back of
1957-58 Hunting License. Owner must
validate by signing name across face
of Stamp.   59593 7-57 500 SPO

Fee $5.00   115

STATE OF CALIFORNIA
DEPARTMENT OF FISH AND GAME
SEASONAL PERMIT for
HONEY LAKE
Valid during 1958-59 Waterfowl Season

Stamp must be pasted on back of
1958-59 Hunting License. Owner must
validate by signing name across face
of stamp.   79670 7-58 500 SPO

158

Fee $5.00   **147**

STATE OF CALIFORNIA
DEPARTMENT OF FISH AND GAME
SEASONAL PERMIT for
HONEY LAKE
Valid during 1959-60 Waterfowl Season
Stamp must be pasted on back of
1959-60 Hunting License. Owner must
validate by signing name across face
of stamp.   1284 7-59 500 SPO

1959-60

4    $5 black, *deep yellow* . . . .   —

Fee $5.00   **86**

STATE OF CALIFORNIA
DEPARTMENT OF FISH AND GAME
SEASONAL PERMIT for
HONEY LAKE
Valid during 1960-61 Waterfowl Season
Stamp must be pasted on back of
1960-61 Hunting License. Owner must
validate by signing name across face
of stamp.   25821 8-60 400 SPO

1960-61

5    $5 black . . . .   —

Fee $5.00   **226**

STATE OF CALIFORNIA
DEPARTMENT OF FISH AND GAME
SEASONAL PERMIT for
HONEY LAKE
Valid during 1961-62 Waterfowl Season
Stamp must be pasted on back of
1961-62 Hunting License. Owner must
validate by signing name across face
of stamp.   44267 6-61 450 SPO

1961-62

6    $5 black, *bluish green* . . . .   —

Fee $5.00   **171**

STATE OF CALIFORNIA
DEPARTMENT OF FISH AND GAME
SEASONAL PERMIT for
HONEY LAKE
Valid during 1962-63 Waterfowl Season
Stamp must be pasted on back of
1962-63 Hunting License. Owner must
validate by signing name across face
of stamp.   68464 7-62 450 SPO

1962-63

7    $5 black, *deep yellow* . . . .   —

Fee $5.00   184

STATE OF CALIFORNIA
DEPARTMENT OF FISH AND GAME
SEASONAL PERMIT for
HONEY LAKE
Valid during 1963-64 Waterfowl Season
Stamp must be pasted on back of
1963-64 Hunting License. Owner must
validate by signing name across face
of stamp.   92947 8-63 450 SPO

Fee $6.50 N⁰   100

STATE OF CALIFORNIA
DEPARTMENT OF FISH AND GAME
SEASONAL PERMIT for
HONEY LAKE
Valid during 1964-65 Waterfowl Season
Stamp must be pasted on back of
1964-65 Hunting License. Owner must
validate by signing name across face
of stamp.
27098-800 7-64 550 OSP

Fee $6.50

STATE OF CALIFORNIA
DEPARTMENT OF FISH AND GAME
SEASONAL PERMIT for
HONEY LAKE
Valid during 1965-1966 Waterfowl Season
Stamp must be pasted on back of
1965/1966 Hunting License. Owner must
validate by signing name across face
of stamp.   52762-800 8-65 600 OSP

Fee $6.50   663

STATE OF CALIFORNIA
DEPARTMENT OF FISH AND GAME
SEASONAL PERMIT for
HONEY LAKE
Valid during 1966-67 Waterfowl Season
Stamp must be pasted on back of
1966-1967 Hunting License. Owner must
validate by signing name across face
of stamp.   77116-800 8-66 700 OSP

1963-64

8     $5 black . . . .   —

1964-65

9     $6.50 black, *pink* . . . .   —

1965-66

10     $6.50 black . . . .   —

1966-67

11     $6.50 black, *yellow*, serial
numbers 1-700, printer's
information at bottom
right . . . .   —
   a. serial numbers 701+,
      no printer's informa-
      tion at bottom right . . .   —

CALIFORNIA

Fee $10.00 622
STATE OF CALIFORNIA
DEPARTMENT OF FISH AND GAME
SEASONAL PERMIT for
HONEY LAKE
Valid During 1967-1968 Waterfowl Season
Stamp must be pasted on back of 1967-1968 Hunting License. Owner must validate by signing name across face of stamp.

Fee $10.00 104
STATE OF CALIFORNIA
DEPARTMENT OF FISH AND GAME
SEASONAL PERMIT for
HONEY LAKE
Valid During 1968-69 Waterfowl Season
Stamp must be pasted on back of 1968-69 Hunting License. Owner must validate by signing name across face of stamp.

Fee $10.00 114
STATE OF CALIFORNIA
DEPARTMENT OF FISH AND GAME
SEASONAL PERMIT for
HONEY LAKE
Valid During 1969-70 Waterfowl Season
Stamp must be pasted on back of 1969-70 Hunting License. Owner must validate by signing name across face of stamp.

Fee $15.00 4
STATE OF CALIFORNIA
DEPARTMENT OF FISH AND GAME
SEASONAL PERMIT for
HONEY LAKE
Valid During 1970-71 Waterfowl Season
Stamp must be pasted on back of 1970-71 Hunting License. Owner must validate by signing name across face of stamp.

1967-68
12    $10 black, *pink* ....   —

1968-69
13    $10 black, *blue* ....   —

1969-70
14    $10 black, *green* ....   —

1970-71
15    $15 black, *yellow* ....   —

161

Fee $15.00   48

STATE OF CALIFORNIA
DEPARTMENT OF FISH AND GAME
SEASONAL PERMIT for
HONEY LAKE

Valid During 1971–72 Waterfowl Season
Stamp must be pasted on back of
1971–72. Hunting License. Owner must
validate by signing name across face
of stamp.

Fee $15.00   5

STATE OF CALIFORNIA
DEPARTMENT OF FISH AND GAME
SEASONAL PERMIT for
HONEY LAKE

Valid During 1972–73 Waterfowl Season
Stamp must be pasted on back of
1972–73 Hunting License. Owner must
validate by signing name across face
of stamp.

Fee $15.00   8

STATE OF CALIFORNIA
DEPARTMENT OF FISH AND GAME
SEASONAL PERMIT for
HONEY LAKE

Valid During 1973–74 Waterfowl Season
Stamp must be pasted on back of
1973–74 Hunting License. Owner must
validate by signing name across face
of stamp.

Fee $15.00   888

STATE OF CALIFORNIA
DEPARTMENT OF FISH AND GAME
SEASONAL PERMIT for
HONEY LAKE

Valid During 1974–75 Waterfowl Season
Stamp must be pasted on back of
1974–75 Hunting License. Owner must
validate by signing name across face
of stamp.

1971-72
16    $15 black, *pink* .... —

1972-73
17    $15 black, *blue* .... —

1973-74
18    $15 black, *blue* .... —

1974-75
19    $15 black, *pink* .... —

Fee $15.00   280

STATE OF CALIFORNIA
DEPARTMENT OF FISH AND GAME
SEASONAL PERMIT for
HONEY LAKE

Valid During 1975–76 Waterfowl Season
Stamp must be pasted on back of
1975–76 Hunting License. Owner must
validate by signing name across face
of stamp.

Fee $15.00   618

STATE OF CALIFORNIA
DEPARTMENT OF FISH AND GAME
SEASONAL PERMIT for
HONEY LAKE

Valid During 1976-77 Waterfowl Season
Stamp must be pasted on back of
1976–77 Hunting License. Owner must
validate by signing name across face
of stamp.

Fee $20.00   635

STATE OF CALIFORNIA
DEPARTMENT OF FISH AND GAME
SEASONAL PERMIT for
HONEY LAKE

Valid During 1977-78 Waterfowl Season
Stamp must be pasted on back of
1977–78 Hunting License. Owner must
validate by signing name across face
of stamp.

Fee $20.00   514

STATE OF CALIFORNIA
DEPARTMENT OF FISH AND GAME
SEASONAL PERMIT for
HONEY LAKE

Valid During 1978-79 Waterfowl Season
Stamp must be pasted on back of
1978–79 Hunting License. Owner must
validate by signing name across face
of stamp.

1975-76

20   $15 black, *green* . . . .   —

1976-77

21   $15 black, *yellow* . . . .   —

1977-78

22   $20 black, *blue* . . . .   —

1978-79

23   $20 black, *yellow* . . . .   —

Fee $20.00   503

STATE OF CALIFORNIA
DEPARTMENT OF FISH AND GAME
SEASONAL PERMIT for
HONEY LAKE
Valid During 1979-80 Waterfowl Season

Stamp must be pasted on back of
1979–80 Hunting License. Owner must
validate by signing name across face
of stamp.

1979-80

24    $20 black, *yellow* .... —

Fee $15.00   580

STATE OF CALIFORNIA
DEPARTMENT OF FISH AND GAME
SEASONAL PERMIT for
HONEY LAKE

Valid During 1980-81 Waterfowl Season

Stamp must be pasted on back of 1980-81
Hunting License. Owner must validate by
signing name across face of stamp.

1980-81

25    $15 black, *blue* .... —

Fee $20.00   1

STATE OF CALIFORNIA
DEPARTMENT OF FISH AND GAME
SEASONAL PERMIT for
HONEY LAKE
Valid During 1981-82 Waterfowl Season
Stamp must be pasted on back of 1981-82
Hunting License. Owner must validate
by signing name across face of stamp.

1981-82

26    $20 black, *yellow* .... —

Fee $20.00   496

STATE OF CALIFORNIA
DEPARTMENT OF FISH AND GAME
SEASONAL PERMIT for
HONEY LAKE
Valid During 1982-83 Waterfowl Season
Stamp must be pasted on back of
1982–83 Hunting License. Owner
must validate by signing name
across face of stamp.

1982-83

27    $20 black, *pink* .... —

Fee $20.00 **593**
STATE OF CALIFORNIA
DEPARTMENT OF FISH AND GAME
SEASONAL PERMIT for
HONEY LAKE
Valid During 1983–84 Waterfowl Season
Stamp must be pasted on back of 1983–84 Hunting License. Owner must validate by signing name across face of stamp.

1983-84

28   $20 black, *green* . . . .   —

Fee $20.00 **0567**
STATE OF CALIFORNIA
DEPARTMENT OF FISH AND GAME
SEASONAL PERMIT for
HONEY LAKE
Valid During 1984–85 Waterfowl Season
Stamp must be pasted on back of 1984–85 Hunting License. Owner must validate by signing name across face of stamp.

1984-85

29   $20 black, *yellow* . . . .   —

Fee $20.00 **0186**
STATE OF CALIFORNIA
DEPARTMENT OF FISH AND GAME
SEASONAL PERMIT for
HONEY LAKE
Valid During 1985–86 Waterfowl Season
Stamp must be pasted on back of 1985–86 Hunting License. Owner must validate by signing name across face of stamp.

1985-86

30   $20 black, *blue* . . . .   —

COLORADO

NORTH CENTRAL GOOSE PERMIT NO. **13202**
COLORADO WILDLIFE COMMISSION
$2.00
1973
This permit not valid unless signed above and attached to the front lower right corner of a current small game license.

North Central Goose Stamp.

1973

1	$2 black, self-adhesive with glassine backing	—

Shown at 70% of original size

KANSAS

Marion County resident duck stamps.
All stamps are text, with
various roulette and perforation gauges.

25c   25c
RESIDENT
DUCK STAMP
1946
Marion County
Park & Lake
25c   25c
KANSAS

*   25c   25c   *
RESIDENT
DUCK STAMP
1947
Marion County
Park & Lake
25c   25c
*   KANSAS   *

1943

1	25c black, *pink*	—

1944

2	25c black, *green*	—

1946

3	25c black, *yellow*	—

1947

4	25c black, *pink*	—

1950

5	50c black, *green*	—

1951

6	50c black, *green*	—

50c	50c
RESIDENT DUCK STAMP 1954 Marion County Park and Lake	
50c	50c

1954

7   50c black, *pink* . . . .   —

50c	50c
RESIDENT Duck Stamp 1955 **Marion County Park and Lake**	
50c	50c

1955

8   50c black, *green* . . . .   —

50c	50c
RESIDENT DUCK STAMP 1956 Marion County Park and Lake	
50c	50c

1956

9   50c black . . . .   —

50c	50c
RESIDENT Duck Stamp 1957 Marion County Park and Lake	
50c	50c

1957

10   50c black, *blue* . . . .   —

```
★----------------★
 50c          50c
   RESIDENT
   Duck Stamp
      1958
  Marion County
  Park and Lake
 50c          50c
★----------------★
```

```
‖ 50c        50c ‖
   RESIDENT
   Duck Stamp
      1959
  Marion   County
  Park  and  Lake
 50c          50c ‖
```

```
●----------------●
 50c          50c
   RESIDENT
   Duck Stamp
      1960
  Marion   County
  Park  and  Lake
 50c          50c
●----------------●
```

```
 50c          50c
   RESIDENT
   Duck Stamp
      1961
  Marion County
  Park and Lake
 50c          50c
```

1958

11   50c black, *yellow* .... —

1959

12   50c black .... —

1960

13   50c black, *pink* .... —

1961

14   50c black .... —

1962

15 50c black .... —

1963

16 50c black, *pink* .... —

1964

17 50c black, *pink* .... —

1965

18 50c black, *green* .... —

50c   50c
RESIDENT
Duck Stamp
1966

Marion County
Park and Lake
50c   50c

50c   50c
RESIDENT
Duck Stamp
1967
Marion County
Park and Lake
50c   50c

50c   50c
RESIDENT
Duck Stamp
1968
Marion County
Park and Lake
50c   50c

50c   50c
RESIDENT
1969
Duck Stamp
Marion County
Park and Lake
50c   50c

1966

19   50c black, *yellow* . . . .   —

1967

20   50c black, *green* . . . .   —

1968

21   50c black, *pink* . . . .   —

1969

22   50c black, *yellow* . . . .   —

```
┌─────────────────────┐
│ 50c          50c    │
│    RESIDENT         │
│      1970           │
│   Duck Stamp        │
│  Marion County      │
│  Park and Lake      │
│ 50c          50c    │
└─────────────────────┘
```

1970

23   50c black .... —

```
┌─────────────────────┐
│ 50c          50c    │
│    RESIDENT         │
│      1971           │
│   Duck Stamp        │
│  Marion County      │
│  Park and Lake      │
│ 50c          50c    │
└─────────────────────┘
```

1971

24   50c black, *pink* .... —

```
┌─────────────────────┐
│ 50c          50c    │
│    RESIDENT         │
│      1972           │
│   Duck Permit       │
│  Marion County      │
│  Park and Lake      │
│ 50c          50c    │
└─────────────────────┘
```

1972

25   50c black, *blue* .... —

```
┌─────────────────────┐
│ 50c          50c    │
│    RESIDENT         │
│      1973           │
│   Duck Permit       │
│  Marion County      │
│  Park and Lake      │
│ 50c          50c    │
└─────────────────────┘
```

1973

26   50c black, *pink* .... —

MINNESOTA

Issued in sheets of 10.
This served as a one dollar surcharge
to cover the cost of a license increase.

1957

1    $1 Mallard & pheasant . . . . .   —

OHIO

Pymatuning Lake waterfowl hunting.

1938

1    $1 black, *yellow,* state seal . .   —

1939-44 stamps may exist.

1945

2    $1 black, *buff,* state seal . . . .   —

```
    1974    FREE    1974
         STATE OF
       SOUTH DAKOTA
BENNETT COUNTY CANADA GOOSE
           328
   OCT. 26 — NOV. 8, 1974
  Game, Fish & Parks Commission
```

```
     1975    FREE    1975
          STATE OF
        SOUTH DAKOTA
BENNETT COUNTY CANADA GOOSE
            267
    OCT. 25 — NOV. 16, 1975
     Game, Fish & Parks
```

```
   1976  FREE  1976
       STATE OF
     SOUTH DAKOTA
    BENNETT COUNTY
     CANADA GOOSE
         413
  NOV. 6 – NOV. 28, 1976
```

```
   1977  FREE  1977
       STATE OF
     SOUTH DAKOTA
        BENNETT COUNTY
297     CANADA GOOSE

  OCT. 15 – OCT. 30, 1977
  NOV. 19 – NOV. 30, 1977
```

Bennett County Canada goose stamps.
Rubber-stamped overprints make
these items valid for use in the county
noted by the overprint.

1974

1   ''Free'' small flying goose,
        black, imperf. . . . .   —
Stamp shown at 70% of original size

1975

2   ''Free'' small flying goose,
        black, *pink*, imperf. . . . . . .   —
Stamp shown at 70% of original size

1976

3   ''Free'' small flying goose,
        black, *blue*, perf. 12,
        booklet single (from
        pane of 5) . . . .   —

1977

4   ''Free'' small flying goose,
        black, *yellow*, perf. 12,
        booklet single (from
        pane of 5) . . . .   —

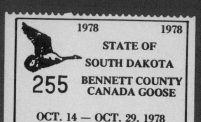

1978

5    $5 Small flying goose, black, *greenish blue*, perf. 12, booklet single (from pane of 5) . . . .   —

1979

6    $2 small flying goose, black, *yellow*, perf. 12, booklet single (from pane of 5) rubber-stamped overprint "Bennett County" . .   —
      a. "Haakon County" . . . . .   —
      b. "Jackson County" . . . . .   —
      c. "Pennington County" .   —
      d. without overprint . . . .   —

Stamps overprinted "Perkins County" exist, but were never issued. The overprint was applied in 1980 to a group of previously un-overprinted items. "Perkins County" over-prints were being applied to 1980 stamps at the same time of the request for stamping onto the 1979 items. There appears to have been no intent to have 1979 stamps with the "Perkins County" overprint.

1980

7    $2 small flying goose, black, *blue*, perf. 12, booklet single (from pane of 5) rubber-stamped over-print "Bennett County" . . . . . .   —
      a. "Haakon County" . . . . .   —
      b. "Jackson County" . . . . .   —
      c. as b, missing serial number . . . .   —
      d. "Pennington County" .   —
      e. "Perkins County" . . . . .   —
      f. without overprint . . . . .   —

1981

8    $2 black text, *red,* inscribed "Prairie Canada Geese," perf. 12, booklet single, (from pane of 5) rubber-stamped overprint "Bennett County" ...... —
    a. "Haakon County" ..... —
    b. "Jackson County" ..... —
    c. "Pennington County" . —
    d. "Perkins County" ..... —
    e. without overprint .... —

1982

9    $2 black, *blue,* all text, inscribed "Prairie Canada Geese," perf. 12, booklet single (from pane of 5), rubber-stamped overprint "Bennett County"........... —
    a. "Haakon County" ..... —
    b. "Jackson County" ..... —
    c. "Pennington County" . —
    d. "Perkins County" ..... —
    e. without overprint .... —

Prairie counties Canada goose stamps.

1983

1    $2 black, *yellow,* all text, perf. 12, booklet single (from pane of 5) rubber-stamped overprint "Unit 2A.".................. —
    a. as above, perf. 9½ .... —
    b. "Unit 11," perf. 12 .... —
    c. as b, perf. 9½ .... —
    d. "Unit 23," perf. 12 .... —
    e. as d, perf. 9½ .... —
    f. "Unit 31," perf. 12 ..... —
    g. as f, perf. 9½ .... —
    h. "Unit 39," perf. 12 .... —
    i. as h, perf. 9½ .... —
    j. "Unit 49," perf. 12 .... —
    k. as j, perf. 9½ .... —
    l. "Unit 53," perf 12 ..... —
    m. as l, perf. 9½ .... —
    n. without overprint, perf. 12.............. —
    o. as n, perf 9½ .... —

1984

2    $2 black, *green,* perf. 12, booklet single (from pane of 5), rubber-stamped overprint "Unit 11" . —
    a. "Unit 23" .... —
    b. "Unit 47" .... —
    c. "Unit 53" .... —
    d. without overprint .... —

Pheasant restoration. These stamps were required to hunt all small game.

1977

1	$5 Pheasant	8.00

1978

2	$5 Pheasant	8.00

1979

3	$5 Pheasant	8.00

1980

4	$5 Pheasant	8.00

1981

5	$5 Pheasant	8.00

1982

6    $5 Pheasant 8.00

1983

7    $5 Pheasant 8.00

1984

8    $5 Pheasant 8.00

1985

9    $5 Pheasant 8.00

1986

| 10 | $5 Pheasant .... | 8.00 |

1987

| 11 | $5 Pheasant .... | 8.00 |

1988

| 12 | $5 Pheasant .... | 8.00 |

SOUTH DAKOTA

```
┌┅┅┅┅┅┅┅┅┅┅┅┅┅┅┅┅┅┅┅┅┅┐
│                                      │
│  LOWER BRULE RESERVATION             │
│   Migratory   Waterfowl              │
│        Permit                        │
│  № ___      159                      │
│                                      │
│  FEE_____  YEAR_____             │
│                                      │
└┅┅┅┅┅┅┅┅┅┅┅┅┅┅┅┅┅┅┅┅┅┘
```

Lower Brule Indian Reservation migratory waterfowl stamps. All stamps have printed text, red serial numbers and provisions for rubber-stamped or handwritten fee (face value) and validity period.

1962

| 1 | $2.50 black | — |
| 2 | $5 black | — |

1963

| 3 | $2.50 black | — |
| 4 | $5 black | — |

1964

| 5 | $2.50 black | — |
| 6 | $5 black | — |

1965

| 7 | $2.50 black | — |
| 8 | $5 black | — |

1966

| 9 | $2.50 black | — |
| 10 | $5 black | — |

1967

| 11 | $2.50 black | — |
| 12 | $5 black | — |

1968

| 13 | $2.50 black | — |
| 14 | $5 black | — |

1969

| 15 | $2.50 black | — |
| 16 | $5 black | — |

SOUVENIR ITEMS

Official souvenir items issued relative to federal duck stamps.

1960

1   Certificate showing 1959 federal stamp (Scott RW26), signed by U.S. Secretary of the Interior, Frank A. Seaton *750.00*

1961

2   Certificate showing 1960 federal stamp (Scott RW27), unsigned ....   —
       a. signed by U.S. Secretary of the Interior, Stewart Udall ....   —
       b. as No. 2, with added ribbon and legend "we do our share, too" ....   —

1972

3   Certificate showing 1971 federal stamp (Scott RW38) ....   —

1980

4   Certificate showing 1980 federal stamp (Scott RW47) *225.00*

Shown at 20% of original size

5   Certificate without illustration of stamp, used from 1980 through 1983. Size: 5 x 7 inches. Blue on cream stock. 75.00

1984

6   "Regional" certificate featuring large illustration of Scott RW1, with space to attach Scott RW51. Brown on parchment. 75.00

Shown at 20% of original size

1985

7   Commemorative overprint on uncut sheets of Scott RW51, released following expiration date for that stamp. Released in sheets of 120, with vertical and horizontal gutters. Commemorative inscription in selvage; individual stamps identical to regular issue (Philatelic Foundation certificate & penciled initials of official on reverse of commemorative stamp).. . . . . ——

8   "Regional" certificate featuring large illustration of Scott RW1, with space to attach Scott RW52. Blue on blue parchment. 350.00

Shown at 20% of original size

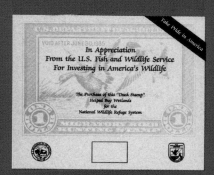

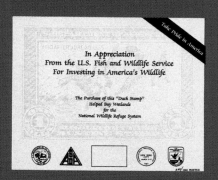

1986

9   Honoring AMERIPEX '86, deep red and blue. Large illustration of Scott RW1 in background. 30.00
Shown at 20% of original size

10   Show card for AMERIPEX '86, showing Statue of Liberty. Issued 5/29/86. .   75.00

11   Show card honoring 100th anniversary of the American Philatelic Society. Issued 8/21/86. .   60.00

12   "Regional" certificate featuring large illustration of Scott RW1, with space to attach Scott RW53. Diagonal Pride in America stripe in upper right. 30.00
Shown at 20% of original size

1987

13   Card, green on sand gray. Pride in America stripe in upper right. Printed for ASDA INTERPEX 87.   —
Shown at 20% of original size

14   "Regional" certificate featuring large illustration of Scott RW1, with space to attach Scott RW54. Brown on light ivory stock. 30.00
     a. brown on ivory stock (believed to be second printing) 30.00

15   Card with Scott RW54 in full color. The Duck Stamp Story printed on reverse. 50.00
     a. Numbered individually (1-200) . . . .   —

1988

16   Card featuring large (one-color) illustration of Scott RW54. Deep red on cream. Printed for ASDA INTERPEX 88. . . . .   30.00

Shown at 20% of original size

17   Similar to above, red on thin white parchment. Printed for WESTPEX 88, San Francisco. 40.00

Shown at 20% of original size

18   Similar to above, blue on thicker ivory. Printed for COMPEX 88, Chicago. . . .   30.00

Shown at 20% of original size

19   Card with Scott RW55 in full color, deep brown on tan with gold foil stamped logos. The Duck Stamp Story printed on reverse 35.00

        a. As above, numbered 101-750 in gold, with first day cancel 85.00

Shown at 20% of original size

20 Card featuring large (one-color) illustration of Scott RW55, print brown on ivory. 30.00
Shown at 20% of original size

21 As above, for BALPEX 88, Baltimore 30.00
Shown at 20% of original size

22 As above, for ASDA NATIONAL 88, New York 20.00
Shown at 20% of original size

23 As above, for INTERPEX 89, New York 20.00
Shown at 20% of original size

24   As above, for WESTPEX 89,
San Francisco 20.00
Shown at 20% of original size

25   As above, for COMPEX 89,
Chicago 20.00
Shown at 20% of original size

GOVERNOR'S EDITIONS

State "Governor's Edition" duck stamps.

ALASKA
1989

5-G $5 Goldeneyes 175.00
        a. signed by governor of
           state 300.00

ARIZONA
1989

3-G $5.50 + $50 Cinnamon teal . 65.00
        a. signed by governor of
           state 175.00

LOUISIANA
1989

1-G $5 Blue-winged teal
      (resident) 165.00
        a. signed by governor of
           state 275.00
2-G $7.50 Blue-winged teal
      (non-resident) 165.00
        a. signed by governor of
           state 275.00

MONTANA
1989

11-G $5 Black Labrador retriever
      & pintail 175.00
        a. signed by governor of
           state 300.00